INNER QUEEN

NO ORDINARY JOURNAL

STEP INTO YOUR POWER, UNLEASH YOUR MAGIC & SET YOURSELF FREE

First Printing, 2020

ISBN 979-8-6134-6717-4

"Your Inner Queen is the highest version of yourself.
She's the real you and goes far beyond the physical
form you've come to believe is your identity.
She knows your purpose and will guide you towards
your deepest desires through intuition and inspiration.
She is your greatest teacher, and with her guidance you will
always be led away from fear and towards joy,
inner peace and unconditional love. Listen to her,
because trust me – she knows where it's at."

Hey Queen,

Welcome to your brand spanking new journal. If right now you're feeling a little disconnected and lost, or like you just don't have your shit together yet…then fear not, the guidance you were looking for is in your hands. These pages hold the power to completely shift your reality and support you as you upgrade your entire life. Our mission as we pieced together this journal, was to create a self-help tool that would act as your very own life coach. One that you can carry around in your handbag and reach for at any given moment; to document your journey and look to for guidance as you rise up to become the fierce, strong, capable Queen that you truly are.

We really want you to feel as though we are with you, cheering you on, empowering you to level up and step more and more into your power every single day. We hope that our positive spirit and kind, encouraging way of speaking to you through these pages inspires you to do the same for yourself. The goal really is to become your own best friend, and to show up as your number one fan – every single day. If you commit to walking the path of deep self-discovery, you'll find that every time the sneaky little voice of self-doubt tries to tear you down, another (much louder) voice from your Inner Queen will interrupt and roar about how utterly enough you are. And when your Inner Queen becomes your default setting, you will become absolutely unstoppable.

One thing you should know about Wendy and I, is that we really have both been through some really painful and challenging experiences. We've felt lost, lonely, confused, doubtful and anxious. We have questioned our purpose, desperately searched for meaning in our own lives, and had our fair share of *sobbing in the bath wondering where it all went wrong* moments. But over the years, we have been fiercely committed to our growth. We have invested thousands in books and courses for our own self development, and we've spent all of our time applying the knowledge we've collected, practising it daily in our own lives. You see, you can devour the entire self-help section of your local bookstore but if you don't actually apply the knowledge and live the teachings, you never really learned it at all. By consistently working on our mindset every single day, we've managed to leave the jobs and relationships that were suffocating us and holding us back. We have become our own best friends and absolutely mastered our inner self-talk. We have stepped into our power, manifested our hearts desires, and proven that when you truly know your worth as a human being – the Universe has no option but to meet you there and reflect this back at you in all areas of your magnificent life. You see, when you finally re-connect to your Inner Queen, life has no choice but to level up alongside you. And the best part? It all starts from within. This gets us super excited, because it's a huge relief to know that the endless and exhausting race to finding happiness through external validation and the accumulation of 'things' ends right here, right now. Nothing you are seeking is outside of you. Not peace, confidence, fulfilment or happiness. You can't win it, buy it, beg, borrow or steal it, because It's been within you all along. You've simply been looking in the wrong direction.

It's time to turn your attention within.

Everything you want to become, you already are. Your Inner Queen is buried under layers and layers of fear that you've picked up over the years by taking on the ideas and beliefs of the people around you. In the pages that follow, we will guide you through worksheets as you unravel the stories that are keeping you bound by invisible shackles and holding you back from the juicy, full-up life you yearn for.

This journal serves as a daily reminder of just how utterly incredible you are and will keep you on the straight and narrow (spiritually speaking) to ensure that you don't get distracted by drama and people/situations that do not serve your highest good. If you show up every day and follow the guidance provided, your life will soon begin to take a magical turn for the better, and you will begin to see some massive changes happening right before your eyes. There are nuggets of potential buried deep within you, just waiting to be discovered so that you can finally grow into the woman you were always destined to become. It is your birth right to feel liberated, worthy, joyful, peaceful and whole. It's time to grab life by the balls and wholeheartedly choose how you want your time on this earth to turn out. It's time to stop letting life happen to you…and start happening to life. My love, you really are the creator of your reality. The power is in your hands, and you've absolutely got this.

Before we embark upon this adventure towards your epic new life, (you know the one where you're fully aligned with your Inner Queen, totally in love with who you are as a person and basking joyfully in the unlimited freedom and abundance this Universe has to offer?) We have to get a little uncomfortable. We need clarity, and for that we must shine a big, brilliant light on your current life situation. There is no judgment here. No hiding, no shame, no guilt. We welcome vulnerability, openness and total honesty. In order to heal and move forward, we have to take a look at why you're shrinking yourself, playing so small and cowering in the corner of your own existence, fuelled by self-doubt and the fear of being seen. Owning your shit is unbelievably powerful, and an incredibly necessary part of your personal transformation.

Once upon a time you were an innocent little human, running around without a care in the world. Full of light, full of spirit and connected to the Universe in a way that was so pure, true and so incredibly trusting. Have you ever noticed the way young children prance around in silly outfits, singing at the top of their lungs, dancing off-beat without an ounce of self-doubt in sight? They stand fully in their power; not one thought about whether they're good enough even comes close to crossing their mind. Little people are always the first ones on the dancefloor, shaking what their Mama gave them. But the adults? After much persuasion and a few glasses of wine they may perform a reserved two-step before swiftly sitting back down and retreating to safety.

As children, we are left untouched by the world for some time. We haven't yet been subjected to the fearful opinions and beliefs of others and if given the privilege, we're often protected by the adults around us. We are encouraged to be and do and have whatever we dream of. The world is our oyster, until one day, something or someone comes along and tells us that we are doing it wrong. We are too loud, too confident. We are told to be quiet, stay silent, turn off our magic and hide our brilliance.

Just take a moment now to think back to a time in your life when someone, or something lead you to believe that you weren't quite good enough. The memory might spring to mind immediately, or it may take a few moments to reveal itself. Don't be surprised if multiple incidents come to mind – this is perfectly normal. Often these seemingly insignificant events sneak their way into our lives and go completely unnoticed, but somehow manage to impact our decisions in a way that ultimately changes the entire course of our lives.

Use the space below to list any memories that came to mind.

....

....

....

....

....

....

....

....

....

....

....

....

....

....

As humans, we take these events and create stories and limiting beliefs about ourselves, our lives and the world around us. These beliefs show up in all areas; from confidence, finance and relationships, to health, spirituality and beyond. If there's an area of your life that isn't working in your favour, you can bet there's a whole library of limiting beliefs to support the reason why. It's time to discover your own. Be honest and write with an open heart.

"Beliefs have the power to create and the power to destroy.
Human beings have the awesome ability to take any
experience of their lives and create a meaning that
disempowers them or one that can literally save their lives."

—Tony Robbins—

List at least 3 limiting beliefs that are holding you back from living your best life.

....

....

....

....

....

....

....

....

....

Your limiting beliefs directly affect the choices you make on a day-to-day basis. Write down at least 3 examples of how you act, based on the beliefs you've written above.

....

....

....

....

....

....

....

....

....

....

....

....

Let's zoom out and look at the bigger picture.

The world really IS your oyster, and believe it or not, you have the power to create any reality you choose. Any resistance you felt when reading that sentence is merely the voice of your limiting beliefs trying to convince you that you're not worth it.

But hey, here's an idea... You do not have to believe everything your mind tells you.

From now on whenever you hear a fearful thought in your mind, you can actively choose NOT to believe it. You have our permission to call bullshit on your own mind.

It's time to rewrite the story of your life. Are you ready to use the power of your imagination? (This is the part where you shout YAAS QUEEN out loud. We don't care if you're in public.)

Take a deep breath, close your eyes and imagine how your life would look if you had absolutely no limits. Where do you live? Which country are you in? Who are you with? How do you feel? What does your ideal day look like? Do not hold back. Nothing is too wild. Write it all down.

....

....

....

....

....

....

....

....

Now smile, because everything you've written above is absolutely possible for you. Your current limiting beliefs have created your current reality, so first we must re-write your beliefs in order for you to align with your new future. Let's manifest this shit.

Write down at least 3 new and empowering beliefs to support the life of your dreams.

....

....

....

....

....

....

....

....

....

"No one saves us but ourselves. No one can and no one may. We ourselves must walk the path."

—Buddha—

It's yours if you want it, but first you must do the work. This will not happen overnight. Growth takes time. But do not let that dishearten you, because the beauty is in the process. This journal is a commitment to yourself, and as much as we would love to, we can't fill these pages for you.

We are here to guide you back towards the truth of who you really are, but it's up to you to show up and create your new life. Don't forget that there's an entire section entitled 'Wobbles' at the back of this journal to help you through any situations or challenges that may try to trip you up or throw you off track. Life happens, shit will hit the fan, but how you handle it is what truly counts. The Wobble guide will help you to step away from fear, guide you back into alignment with your Inner Queen, and remind you that you can handle absolutely anything. You are so much stronger than you could ever know, and we believe in you with our whole hearts.

The Purpose of this Journal

This journal will provide you with the self-awareness, intention and daily routine required to change your life. If you show up everyday then the habit of filling these pages will become ingrained within you. Putting pen to paper will come as easily and naturally as brushing your teeth. So here's a little guide to the journaling pages ahead:

Morning Inspiration

- Checking in with yourself as soon as you rise should be your top priority. Self-awareness is the foundation on which we create lasting change, and getting super honest about how you're feeling is the best place to start. From here you can decide how to approach the rest of your day with self-compassion and focused intention.

- Taking three deep breaths is the perfect way to ground yourself, release any tension you may have carried over from the day before and bring a sense of connection and calmness in to your mind and body. Smiling releases endorphins and will help you to feel good, raising your vibration. Don't skip this step!

- Affirmations quite literally reprogramme our brains and help to combat subconscious negative self-talk. They will bring forward the voice of your Inner Queen and by practising them everyday you will be slowly but surely changing your inner dialogue. The goal is to become your own best friend, so choose empowering, kind, and motivating affirmations that feel good. If they don't feel good, it may be that you've chosen something a little too far removed from your current beliefs. If you're feeling lost and confused, the affirmation "I have total clarity" will be too ambitious. Instead choose something a little softer such as, "The fog is starting to clear and I am finding more clarity."

- Your Inner Queen has the answer to every single one of your questions, her advice always comes from a place of love and compassion and by tuning into her wisdom she will help you to overcome your fears and perceived problems. Her voice is quiet, and it takes us to slow down and really listen in order to hear what she has to say. Take a moment to close your eyes and receive her guidance.

- Gratitude is your greatest super power. Feeling truly grateful creates such a high vibe energy, which completely transforms your life because it's the key to attracting more of good stuff. The more grateful you are, the more flows in. Even if your life circumstances are difficult right now, there are always things to be grateful for. You woke up today. You have access to running water, food and clothing. Close your eyes and really take a moment to appreciate how lucky you are for even the most simple of things.

- Action is important. But what's even more important is that you are taking action from a place of love and inspiration. What choices can you make to ensure the day ahead is uplifting, enjoyable and intentional? If you're feeling overwhelmed, you've committed to too much and you need a break – your inspired action maybe to do less, meditate, or go to the spa. If you're feeling uninspired it maybe that you need to get out in nature and spend some time with your bare feet on the ground. Remember, action doesn't always have to be fast paced.

- Facing setbacks is a natural and necessary part of human life. Everyday we experience challenges and unexpected mishaps. Maybe you'll miss the bus, spill your coffee, or an argument with your spouse will attempt to lower your vibration. The way we handle these obstacles is what defines where we're at with our level of self-awareness and ability to remain calm and loving during moments of confrontation. Your Inner Queen will always choose the path of least resistance, so instead of arguing with reality – take a moment to plan ahead and choose how you will handle setbacks with grace, kindness and respect.

- In a world where we are constantly trying to achieve more and strive for success, it's very rare that we take a moment to sit back and really smell the roses. When was the last time you celebrated both your small and big wins? You've already achieved so much over the course of your life, but success means nothing if you're not present enough to notice and delight in it. From now on, you'll be celebrating yourself every day. Give yourself a round of applause or a pat on the back; take yourself out for lunch, go for a walk in the park without your phone and just think about everything you've achieved. It can be simple – what's important is that you take the time to appreciate yourself and all that you're doing.

Daily Queen Habits

Movement – Whether it's a walk in the park, a 10 minute morning stretch, dancing around the living room to Beyoncé or getting off the bus a few stops early and walking the rest of the way; getting some movement into your day is such a gift to yourself. If you have the privilege of being able to move your body – do not take it for granted.

Stillness – Take a moment each day to just sit with yourself and breathe deeply. Whether you choose to sit with your eyes closed, take a seat in the park with no distractions, hang out in nature or do a guided meditation, stillness will deepen the connection with your Inner Queen. It's the ultimate path to inner peace, so keep showing up until it becomes a habit.

Kindness – Our Inner Queen knows that we really do rise by lifting others. The more we can do to support each other, the more beautiful the world will become. Kindness has a snowball effect, and by raising your vibration through compassion and selflessness you are raising the vibration of collective consciousness. From giving a compliment, holding a door open, talking to the person next to you on public transport or buying a homeless person a coffee, there are so many ways we can pay it forward.

Evening Reflection

- Checking in with yourself in the evening is a great way to reflect upon how your day unfolded. If you're feeling worse than you did this morning, why is that? What can you do differently tomorrow? If you're feeling better, why is that? What did you do to help yourself, and how can you repeat this more often?

- It's so important and pause for a moment and acknowledge your big wins. It could be that you handled conflict well, made a new friend, received a promotion or enjoyed a really delicious lunch. Whatever it is – write it down and take a moment to be grateful.

- Lessons play the most significant role in our growth, and it's important to acknowledge these too. Please never see a lesson as negative, even if a moment of adversity felt difficult at the time, it always has something to teach us and can therefore be turned into a positive. What did you learn today?

The Inspired Action Page can be used as a diary, a daily planner or a place to write or draw freely – whatever feels right, sparks joy and gets your creative juices flowing.

"Showing up is essential. Showing up consistently is powerful. Showing up consistently with a positive outlook is even more powerful."

—Jeff Olson—

Take three long deep breaths and smile.

Date: 01 / 04 / 2020   **Time I woke up:** 5.45am

How would you rate your mood this morning? 0 1 2 3 4 ⑤ 6 7 8 9 10

Choose three power affirmations to raise your vibration:

♛ I am capable of change

♛ I am loved

♛ I deserve to follow my heart and dream big!

Your Inner Queen always has a message for you.
Which words of encouragement does she need you to hear today?

♛ You are worth listening to! Don't be afraid to speak up today.

The world is a beautiful place. List three reasons to be grateful today:

♛ I am grateful for a new day

♛ I am grateful for lunch plans with Beth today

♛ I am grateful I am well today

Choose three inspired actions to make today amazing:

♛ Find a new podcast and listen to one episode

♛ Unfollow every account on social media that makes me feel bad

♛ Put my phone on flight mode at 9pm tonight

If something tries to trip you up today, how will your Inner Queen handle it?

♛ She will pause, breathe and take a minute before reacting

How will you celebrate yourself today?

♛ I will smile every time I see my reflection today

Evening Reflection

How would you rate your mood this evening? 0 1 2 3 4 5 6 7 ⑧ 9 10

Today's big win: I spoke at my meeting confidently

Today's big lesson: My confidence grows when I put it in practice!!!

13

'Never bend your head. Always hold it high. Look the world straight in the eye'

—*Helen Keller*—

Daily Queen Habits

☑ MOVEMENT   ☑ STILLNESS   ☑ KINDNESS

6am   *Meditate (stillness)*..................   1pm   ....

7am   ....   2pm   *Send Mum a text to say you are*
                                                   grateful for her (kindness)

8am   ....   3pm   ....

9am   ....   4pm   ....

10am   ....   5pm   ....

11am   ....   6pm   *Listen to podcast while cooking*..

12pm   *Go for short walk (movement)*....   7pm   ....

....

....

....

....

....

....

....

....

....

....

....

....

....

Life Assessment

Rate where you feel you are in each area right now
(1 being low vibration and 10 being high vibe!)

Energy   ① 2 3 4 5 6 7 8 9 10
I feel energised, healthy and I'm moving my body regularly.

Mental Health   ① 2 3 4 5 6 7 8 9 10
I am compassionate towards myself and have a kind, uplifting inner dialogue.

Relationships/Love   1 ② 3 4 5 6 7 8 9 10
I have a deep, meaningful and healthy connection with my partner. My relationship brings me joy and fulfilment. (If single: I have a deep, meaningful and healthy connection with myself. I nurture myself and show myself love.)

Purpose   ① 2 3 4 5 6 7 8 9 10
I am finding my purpose in this world. I am committed to feeling fulfilled and excited by my life. I follow my heart and listen to my inner guidance.

Circle   1 2 3 4 5 6 7 ⑧ 9 10
I am surrounded by uplifting, supportive people who raise me higher and inspire me to be the best version of myself.

Self Care   ① 2 3 4 5 6 7 8 9 10
I spend time taking care of myself, allowing myself to rest and recover and treat myself with loving kindness.

Connection   ① 2 3 4 5 6 7 8 9 10
I feel a deep sense of connection to my Inner Queen. I understand that I am always being supported by the Universe and can ask for help and guidance whenever I need it.

Abundance   ① 2 3 4 5 6 7 8 9 10
I see abundance all around me and understand that the Universe is overflowing with everything I could ever need to thrive. I am generous because I know that there is always enough to go around. I am open to receiving all of the goodness life has to offer.

Growth   ① 2 3 4 5 6 7 8 9 10
I have the courage to try new things and pursue my dreams everyday. I use adversity to learn, grow and adapt, and I understand that growth is an integral part of my journey.

Change is possible for all of us.
We believe in you.

Date: 11 / 09 20   Time I woke up: 07:30

How would you rate your mood this morning? 0 1 (2) 3 4 5 6 7 8 9 10

Choose three power affirmations to raise your vibration:
- I am capable of changing my habits
- I can achieve happiness
- I will feel confidant again

Your Inner Queen always has a message for you.
Which words of encouragement does she need you to hear today?
- You are enough

The world is a beautiful place. List three reasons to be grateful today:
- Isla is healthy + happy
- I have a roof over my head
- I am healthy + well

Choose three inspired actions to make today amazing:
- Call w/ Roxie
- Exercise
- write letter to myself.

If something tries to trip you up today, how will your Inner Queen handle it?
- breathe! Count to 10.

How will you celebrate yourself today?
- ~~smile~~ smile when I look in the mirror

Evening Reflection

How would you rate your mood this evening? 0 1 2 3 4 5 (6) 7 8 9 10

Today's big win: Call w/ Roxie

Today's big lesson: I am the only person who can change my future.

'Never bend your head. Always hold it high. Look the world straight in the eye'

—Helen Keller—

Daily Queen Habits

☐ MOVEMENT ☐ STILLNESS ☐ KINDNESS

6am	1pm
7am	2pm
8am	3pm
9am	4pm
10am	5pm
11am	6pm
12pm	7pm

Positivity journal

1. ~~~~ The waiter @ Carluccios was v. smiley
2. I had a lovely phone call w/ Clare & Sophie
3. Isla was so pleased to see me after nursery
4. She ate all her lunch
5. I had a great convo w/Rosie
6. ~~She~~ Isla giggled so much on the sofa that it made my heart hurt.

Take three long deep breaths and smile.

Rich got up
— with
Isla!!

Date: 24 / 11 / 20   Time I woke up: 07.00

How would you rate your mood this morning? 0 1 2 3 4 ⑤ 6 7 8 9 10

Choose three power affirmations to raise your vibration:

♔ My body is beautiful + grew my baby

♔ I am a wonderful partner

♔ I can ~~do~~ achieve whatever I want this week.

Your Inner Queen always has a message for you.
Which words of encouragement does she need you to hear today?

♔ You will commit to a healthier lifestyle for you + your family

The world is a beautiful place. List three reasons to be grateful today:

♔ Isla is healthy + happy

♔ We have a beautiful roof over our heads

♔ Rich + I both have our jobs post the pandemic

Choose three ~~inspired actions to make today amazing:~~ 3 things I did

♔ found a workout + completed it

♔ Did a bedtime yoga routine

♔ Cooked dinner for my husband to be

If something tries to trip you up today, how will your Inner Queen handle it?

♔ Breathe with james

How will you celebrate yourself today?

♔ Exercise

Evening Reflection

How would you rate your mood this evening? 0 1 2 3 4 5 6 7 ⑧ 9 10

Today's big win: starting my exercise regime

Today's big lesson: I have more grit than I think

19

Daily Queen Habits

☐ MOVEMENT   ☐ STILLNESS   ☐ KINDNESS

6am	1pm ....
7am	2pm Movement
8am	3pm ....
9am	4pm ....
10am	5pm ....
11am	6pm ....
12pm	7pm Movement

I ~~feel~~ want to shift my low mood to make our house more joyful. I want Isla to remember her childhood with her Mummy + daddy happy + playful. It makes me frustrated that I have everything I ever dreamed of but I still feel lost. I need to reconnect + find time for self love + self care w/out judging + berating myself. I will do this by moving my body in some way everyday + eating well. Take vitamins + drink 2L of water p/day to reduce headaches.

20

Take three long deep breaths and smile.

Date: /   /   Time I woke up:

How would you rate your mood this morning? 0 1 2 3 4 5 6 7 8 9 10

Choose three power affirmations to raise your vibration:

♛ ....

♛ ....

♛ ....

Your Inner Queen always has a message for you.
Which words of encouragement does she need you to hear today?

♛ ....

....

The world is a beautiful place. List three reasons to be grateful today:

♛ ....

♛ ....

♛ ....

Choose three inspired actions to make today amazing:

♛ ....

♛ ....

♛ ....

If something tries to trip you up today, how will your Inner Queen handle it?

♛ ....

....

How will you celebrate yourself today?

♛ ....

Evening Reflection

How would you rate your mood this evening? 0 1 2 3 4 5 6 7 8 9 10

Today's big win: ....

Today's big lesson: ....

Daily Queen Habits

I am Grateful for today...

☐ MOVEMENT   ☑ STILLNESS   ☐ KINDNESS

6am

7am   1. Isla's health

8am   2. My family's health

9am   3. Our beautiful new home

10am 4. Model processing my refund

11am 5. A safe space to exercise

12pm 6. Rich for calling me to check in

1pm

2pm

3pm

4pm

5pm

6pm

7pm

Positivity Journal

1. Isla gave me lots of cuddles after nursery

2. I exercised today for the 1st time in months

3. Em's wedding will be amazing

4. The delivery drivers found our house

5. I had a nice, brief chat w/ Tayo

6. Isla had a great day at nursery and ate all her food.

7. I spoke to a lovely lady called Mana.

8. It was good to connect w/ the team @ work.

Take three long deep breaths and smile.

Date: 25 / 11 / 20   Time I woke up:

How would you rate your mood this morning? 0 1 2 3 4 5 6 (7) 8 9 10

Choose three power affirmations to raise your vibration:
- 👑 I am taking control of my mental health
- 👑 I am light + love
- 👑 I am the best Mum to Isla.

Your Inner Queen always has a message for you.
Which words of encouragement does she need you to hear today?
- 👑 You can work, be a mum + practice self care

The world is a beautiful place. List three reasons to be grateful today:
- 👑 I can afford to speak w/ a counsellor
- 👑 I have wonderful friends
- 👑 I can move my body today

Choose three inspired actions to make today amazing:
- 👑 Journal this eve
- 👑 Counselling
- 👑 Exercise

If something tries to trip you up today, how will your Inner Queen handle it?
- 👑 breathe with james.

How will you celebrate yourself today?
- 👑 Have a bath this eve!

Evening Reflection

How would you rate your mood this evening? 0 1 2 3 4 5 6 7 8 9 10

Today's big win:

Today's big lesson:

'You must do the things you think you cannot do.'

—Eleanor Roosevelt—

Daily Queen Habits

☐ MOVEMENT   ☐ STILLNESS   ☐ KINDNESS

6am ....   1pm ....

7am ....   2pm ....

8am ....   3pm ....

9am ....   4pm ....

10am ....   5pm ....

11am ....   6pm ....

12pm ....   7pm ....

....

....

....

....

....

....

....

....

....

....

....

....

Date: 28/11/20   Time I woke up:

How would you rate your mood this morning? 0 1 2 3 4 5 ⑥ 7 8 9 10

Choose three power affirmations to raise your vibration:

♛ I am the best mama to isla

♛ I will make the right decision for our family.

♛ I feel confident + happy

Your Inner Queen always has a message for you.
Which words of encouragement does she need you to hear today?

♛ stop thinking, be present + enjoy the day with Isla.

The world is a beautiful place. List three reasons to be grateful today:

♛ My beautiful family

♛ Rick choosing our wedding music

♛ Seeing family @ Painshill

Choose three inspired actions to make today amazing:

♛ Eat well + w/consciousness

♛ Complete Mooody Stretch routine

♛ Phones down for walk + evening

If something tries to trip you up today, how will your Inner Queen handle it?

♛ Take 5, Grow a gaze!

How will you celebrate yourself today?

♛ A bath after the stretch routine

Evening Reflection

How would you rate your mood this evening? 0 1 2 3 4 5 6 7 8 9 10

Today's big win:

Today's big lesson:

'It isn't where you came from but where you are going that counts'

—Ella Fitzgerald—

Daily Queen Habits

☐ MOVEMENT   ☐ STILLNESS   ☐ KINDNESS

6am ....   1pm ....

7am ....   2pm ....

8am ....   3pm ....

9am ....   4pm ....

10am ....   5pm ....

11am ....   6pm ....

12pm ....   7pm ....

....

....

....

....

....

....

....

....

....

....

....

....

....

Take three long deep breaths and smile.

Date: /   /   Time I woke up:

How would you rate your mood this morning? 0 1 2 3 4 5 6 7 8 9 10

Choose three power affirmations to raise your vibration:

👑 ....

👑 ....

👑 ....

Your Inner Queen always has a message for you.
Which words of encouragement does she need you to hear today?

👑 ....

....

The world is a beautiful place. List three reasons to be grateful today:

👑 ....

👑 ....

👑 ....

Choose three inspired actions to make today amazing:

👑 ....

👑 ....

👑 ....

If something tries to trip you up today, how will your Inner Queen handle it?

👑 ....

....

How will you celebrate yourself today?

👑 ....

Evening Reflection

How would you rate your mood this evening? 0 1 2 3 4 5 6 7 8 9 10

Today's big win: ....

Today's big lesson: ....

'My mission in life is not merely to survive, but to thrive.'

—*Maya Angelou*—

Daily Queen Habits

☐ MOVEMENT ☐ STILLNESS ☐ KINDNESS

6am .... 1pm ....

7am .... 2pm ....

8am .... 3pm ....

9am .... 4pm ....

10am .... 5pm ....

11am .... 6pm ....

12pm .... 7pm ....

....

....

....

....

....

....

....

....

....

....

....

....

Take three long deep breaths and smile.

Date: /   /   Time I woke up:

How would you rate your mood this morning? 0 1 2 3 4 5 6 7 8 9 10

Choose three power affirmations to raise your vibration:

♕ ....

♕ ....

♕ ....

Your Inner Queen always has a message for you.
Which words of encouragement does she need you to hear today?

♕ ....

....

The world is a beautiful place. List three reasons to be grateful today:

♕ ....

♕ ....

♕ ....

Choose three inspired actions to make today amazing:

♕ ....

♕ ....

♕ ....

If something tries to trip you up today, how will your Inner Queen handle it?

♕ ....

....

How will you celebrate yourself today?

♕ ....

Evening Reflection

How would you rate your mood this evening? 0 1 2 3 4 5 6 7 8 9 10

Today's big win: ....

Today's big lesson: ....

'You don't always need a plan. Sometimes you just need
to breathe, trust, let go and see what happens.'

—Mandy Hale—

Daily Queen Habits

☐ MOVEMENT   ☐ STILLNESS   ☐ KINDNESS

6am ....   1pm ....

7am ....   2pm ....

8am ....   3pm ....

9am ....   4pm ....

10am ....   5pm ....

11am ....   6pm ....

12pm ....   7pm ....

....

....

....

....

....

....

....

....

....

....

....

....

Take three long deep breaths and smile.

Date: /   /   Time I woke up:

How would you rate your mood this morning? 0   1   2   3   4   5   6   7   8   9   10

Choose three power affirmations to raise your vibration:

♔ ....

♔ ....

♔ ....

Your Inner Queen always has a message for you.
Which words of encouragement does she need you to hear today?

♔ ....

....

The world is a beautiful place. List three reasons to be grateful today:

♔ ....

♔ ....

♔ ....

Choose three inspired actions to make today amazing:

♔ ....

♔ ....

♔ ....

If something tries to trip you up today, how will your Inner Queen handle it?

♔ ....

....

How will you celebrate yourself today?

♔ ....

Evening Reflection

How would you rate your mood this evening? 0   1   2   3   4   5   6   7   8   9   10

Today's big win: ....

Today's big lesson: ....

Daily Queen Habits

☐ MOVEMENT   ☐ STILLNESS   ☐ KINDNESS

6am	1pm ....
7am	2pm ....
8am	3pm ....
9am	4pm ....
10am	5pm ....
11am	6pm ....
12pm	7pm ....

....

....

....

....

....

....

....

....

....

....

....

....

....

Take three long deep breaths and smile.

Date: /   /   Time I woke up:

How would you rate your mood this morning? 0 1 2 3 4 5 6 7 8 9 10

Choose three power affirmations to raise your vibration:

♛ ....

♛ ....

♛ ....

Your Inner Queen always has a message for you.
Which words of encouragement does she need you to hear today?

♛ ....

....

The world is a beautiful place. List three reasons to be grateful today:

♛ ....

♛ ....

♛ ....

Choose three inspired actions to make today amazing:

♛ ....

♛ ....

♛ ....

If something tries to trip you up today, how will your Inner Queen handle it?

♛ ....

....

How will you celebrate yourself today?

♛ ....

Evening Reflection

How would you rate your mood this evening? 0 1 2 3 4 5 6 7 8 9 10

Today's big win: ....

Today's big lesson: ....

'All our dreams can come true, if we have the courage to pursue them.'

—Walt Disney—

Daily Queen Habits

☐ MOVEMENT   ☐ STILLNESS   ☐ KINDNESS

6am	....	1pm	....
7am	....	2pm	....
8am	....	3pm	....
9am	....	4pm	....
10am	....	5pm	....
11am	....	6pm	....
12pm	....	7pm	....

....
....
....
....
....
....
....
....
....
....
....
....
....

Take three long deep breaths and smile.

Date: /   /   Time I woke up:

How would you rate your mood this morning? 0 1 2 3 4 5 6 7 8 9 10

Choose three power affirmations to raise your vibration:

♔ ....

♔ ....

♔ ....

Your Inner Queen always has a message for you.
Which words of encouragement does she need you to hear today?

♔ ....

....

The world is a beautiful place. List three reasons to be grateful today:

♔ ....

♔ ....

♔ ....

Choose three inspired actions to make today amazing:

♔ ....

♔ ....

♔ ....

If something tries to trip you up today, how will your Inner Queen handle it?

♔ ....

....

How will you celebrate yourself today?

♔ ....

Evening Reflection

How would you rate your mood this evening? 0 1 2 3 4 5 6 7 8 9 10

Today's big win: ....

Today's big lesson: ....

'When you want something, all the universe conspires in helping you to achieve it.'
—*Paulo Coelho*—

Daily Queen Habits

☐ MOVEMENT ☐ STILLNESS ☐ KINDNESS

6am .... 1pm ....

7am .... 2pm ....

8am .... 3pm ....

9am .... 4pm ....

10am .... 5pm ....

11am .... 6pm ....

12pm .... 7pm ....

....

....

....

....

....

....

....

....

....

....

....

....

Take three long deep breaths and smile.

Date: /   /   Time I woke up:

How would you rate your mood this morning? 0 1 2 3 4 5 6 7 8 9 10

Choose three power affirmations to raise your vibration:

♕ ....

♕ ....

♕ ....

Your Inner Queen always has a message for you.
Which words of encouragement does she need you to hear today?

♕ ....

....

The world is a beautiful place. List three reasons to be grateful today:

♕ ....

♕ ....

♕ ....

Choose three inspired actions to make today amazing:

♕ ....

♕ ....

♕ ....

If something tries to trip you up today, how will your Inner Queen handle it?

♕ ....

....

How will you celebrate yourself today?

♕ ....

Evening Reflection

How would you rate your mood this evening? 0 1 2 3 4 5 6 7 8 9 10

Today's big win: ....

Today's big lesson: ....

'You can never cross the ocean unless you have the courage to lose sight of the shore.'

—Christopher Columbus—

Daily Queen Habits

☐ MOVEMENT   ☐ STILLNESS   ☐ KINDNESS

6am ....   1pm ....

7am ....   2pm ....

8am ....   3pm ....

9am ....   4pm ....

10am ....   5pm ....

11am ....   6pm ....

12pm ....   7pm ....

....

....

....

....

....

....

....

....

....

....

....

....

....

Take three long deep breaths and smile.

Date: /   /   Time I woke up:

How would you rate your mood this morning? 0 1 2 3 4 5 6 7 8 9 10

Choose three power affirmations to raise your vibration:

♛ ....

♛ ....

♛ ....

Your Inner Queen always has a message for you.
Which words of encouragement does she need you to hear today?

♛ ....

....

The world is a beautiful place. List three reasons to be grateful today:

♛ ....

♛ ....

♛ ....

Choose three inspired actions to make today amazing:

♛ ....

♛ ....

♛ ....

If something tries to trip you up today, how will your Inner Queen handle it?

♛ ....

....

How will you celebrate yourself today?

♛ ....

Evening Reflection

How would you rate your mood this evening? 0 1 2 3 4 5 6 7 8 9 10

Today's big win: ....

Today's big lesson: ....

39

'Never give up on a dream because of the time it will take, the time will pass anyway.'

—Earl Nightingale—

Daily Queen Habits

☐ MOVEMENT   ☐ STILLNESS   ☐ KINDNESS

6am ....   1pm ....

7am ....   2pm ....

8am ....   3pm ....

9am ....   4pm ....

10am ....   5pm ....

11am ....   6pm ....

12pm ....   7pm ....

....

....

....

....

....

....

....

....

....

....

....

....

....

....

Take three long deep breaths and smile.

Date: /   /   Time I woke up:

How would you rate your mood this morning? 0 1 2 3 4 5 6 7 8 9 10

Choose three power affirmations to raise your vibration:

👑 ....

👑 ....

👑 ....

Your Inner Queen always has a message for you.
Which words of encouragement does she need you to hear today?

👑 ....

....

The world is a beautiful place. List three reasons to be grateful today:

👑 ....

👑 ....

👑 ....

Choose three inspired actions to make today amazing:

👑 ....

👑 ....

👑 ....

If something tries to trip you up today, how will your Inner Queen handle it?

👑 ....

....

How will you celebrate yourself today?

👑 ....

Evening Reflection

How would you rate your mood this evening? 0 1 2 3 4 5 6 7 8 9 10

Today's big win: ....

Today's big lesson: ....

'The more you praise & celebrate your life, the more there is to celebrate.'

—Oprah—

Daily Queen Habits

☐ MOVEMENT   ☐ STILLNESS   ☐ KINDNESS

6am ....   1pm ....

7am ....   2pm ....

8am ....   3pm ....

9am ....   4pm ....

10am ....   5pm ....

11am ....   6pm ....

12pm ....   7pm ....

....

....

....

....

....

....

....

....

....

....

....

....

....

....

Take three long deep breaths and smile.

Date: /   /   Time I woke up:

How would you rate your mood this morning? 0 1 2 3 4 5 6 7 8 9 10

Choose three power affirmations to raise your vibration:

👑 ....

👑 ....

👑 ....

Your Inner Queen always has a message for you.
Which words of encouragement does she need you to hear today?

👑 ....

....

The world is a beautiful place. List three reasons to be grateful today:

👑 ....

👑 ....

👑 ....

Choose three inspired actions to make today amazing:

👑 ....

👑 ....

👑 ....

If something tries to trip you up today, how will your Inner Queen handle it?

👑 ....

....

How will you celebrate yourself today?

👑 ....

Evening Reflection

How would you rate your mood this evening? 0 1 2 3 4 5 6 7 8 9 10

Today's big win: ....

Today's big lesson: ....

'Courage starts with showing up and letting ourselves be seen.'

—Brene Brown—

Daily Queen Habits

☐ MOVEMENT   ☐ STILLNESS   ☐ KINDNESS

6am ....   1pm ....

7am ....   2pm ....

8am ....   3pm ....

9am ....   4pm ....

10am ....   5pm ....

11am ....   6pm ....

12pm ....   7pm ....

....

....

....

....

....

....

....

....

....

....

....

....

....

....

Take three long deep breaths and smile.

Date: /   /   Time I woke up:

How would you rate your mood this morning? 0 1 2 3 4 5 6 7 8 9 10

Choose three power affirmations to raise your vibration:

♛ ....

♛ ....

♛ ....

Your Inner Queen always has a message for you.
Which words of encouragement does she need you to hear today?

♛ ....

....

The world is a beautiful place. List three reasons to be grateful today:

♛ ....

♛ ....

♛ ....

Choose three inspired actions to make today amazing:

♛ ....

♛ ....

♛ ....

If something tries to trip you up today, how will your Inner Queen handle it?

♛ ....

....

How will you celebrate yourself today?

♛ ....

Evening Reflection

How would you rate your mood this evening? 0 1 2 3 4 5 6 7 8 9 10

Today's big win: ....

Today's big lesson: ....

'You cannot be lonely if you like the person you are alone with.'
—Wayne Dyer—

Daily Queen Habits

☐ MOVEMENT   ☐ STILLNESS   ☐ KINDNESS

6am ....
7am ....
8am ....
9am ....
10am ....
11am ....
12pm ....

1pm ....
2pm ....
3pm ....
4pm ....
5pm ....
6pm ....
7pm ....

....
....
....
....
....
....
....
....
....
....
....
....
....
....

Take three long deep breaths and smile.

Date: /   /   Time I woke up:

How would you rate your mood this morning? 0 1 2 3 4 5 6 7 8 9 10

Choose three power affirmations to raise your vibration:

♛ ....

♛ ....

♛ ....

Your Inner Queen always has a message for you.
Which words of encouragement does she need you to hear today?

♛ ....

....

The world is a beautiful place. List three reasons to be grateful today:

♛ ....

♛ ....

♛ ....

Choose three inspired actions to make today amazing:

♛ ....

♛ ....

♛ ....

If something tries to trip you up today, how will your Inner Queen handle it?

♛ ....

....

How will you celebrate yourself today?

♛ ....

Evening Reflection

How would you rate your mood this evening? 0 1 2 3 4 5 6 7 8 9 10

Today's big win: ....

Today's big lesson: ....

'Sometimes you need to slow down to go fast.'

—Jeff Olson—

Daily Queen Habits

☐ MOVEMENT   ☐ STILLNESS   ☐ KINDNESS

6am ....   1pm ....

7am ....   2pm ....

8am ....   3pm ....

9am ....   4pm ....

10am ....   5pm ....

11am ....   6pm ....

12pm ....   7pm ....

....

....

....

....

....

....

....

....

....

....

....

....

....

....

Take three long deep breaths and smile.

Date: /   /   Time I woke up:

How would you rate your mood this morning? 0 1 2 3 4 5 6 7 8 9 10

Choose three power affirmations to raise your vibration:

♕ ....

♕ ....

♕ ....

Your Inner Queen always has a message for you.
Which words of encouragement does she need you to hear today?

♕ ....

....

The world is a beautiful place. List three reasons to be grateful today:

♕ ....

♕ ....

♕ ....

Choose three inspired actions to make today amazing:

♕ ....

♕ ....

♕ ....

If something tries to trip you up today, how will your Inner Queen handle it?

♕ ....

....

How will you celebrate yourself today?

♕ ....

Evening Reflection

How would you rate your mood this evening? 0 1 2 3 4 5 6 7 8 9 10

Today's big win: ....

Today's big lesson: ....

49

'Love is what we are born with. Fear is what we learned here.'

—Marianne Williamson—

Daily Queen Habits

☐ MOVEMENT   ☐ STILLNESS   ☐ KINDNESS

6am ....   1pm ....

7am ....   2pm ....

8am ....   3pm ....

9am ....   4pm ....

10am ....   5pm ....

11am ....   6pm ....

12pm ....   7pm ....

....

....

....

....

....

....

....

....

....

....

....

....

....

....

Take three long deep breaths and smile.

Date: /   /   Time I woke up:

How would you rate your mood this morning? 0 1 2 3 4 5 6 7 8 9 10

Choose three power affirmations to raise your vibration:

👑 ....

👑 ....

👑 ....

Your Inner Queen always has a message for you.
Which words of encouragement does she need you to hear today?

👑 ....

....

The world is a beautiful place. List three reasons to be grateful today:

👑 ....

👑 ....

👑 ....

Choose three inspired actions to make today amazing:

👑 ....

👑 ....

👑 ....

If something tries to trip you up today, how will your Inner Queen handle it?

👑 ....

....

How will you celebrate yourself today?

👑 ....

Evening Reflection

How would you rate your mood this evening? 0 1 2 3 4 5 6 7 8 9 10

Today's big win: ....

Today's big lesson: ....

'A memory without the emotional charge is called wisdom.'

—Joe Dispenza—

Daily Queen Habits

☐ MOVEMENT ☐ STILLNESS ☐ KINDNESS

6am .... 1pm ....

7am .... 2pm ....

8am .... 3pm ....

9am .... 4pm ....

10am .... 5pm ....

11am .... 6pm ....

12pm .... 7pm ....

....

....

....

....

....

....

....

....

....

....

....

....

Take three long deep breaths and smile.

Date: /   /   Time I woke up:

How would you rate your mood this morning? 0 1 2 3 4 5 6 7 8 9 10

Choose three power affirmations to raise your vibration:

♛ ....

♛ ....

♛ ....

Your Inner Queen always has a message for you.
Which words of encouragement does she need you to hear today?

♛ ....

....

The world is a beautiful place. List three reasons to be grateful today:

♛ ....

♛ ....

♛ ....

Choose three inspired actions to make today amazing:

♛ ....

♛ ....

♛ ....

If something tries to trip you up today, how will your Inner Queen handle it?

♛ ....

....

How will you celebrate yourself today?

♛ ....

Evening Reflection

How would you rate your mood this evening? 0 1 2 3 4 5 6 7 8 9 10

Today's big win: ....

Today's big lesson: ....

*'What other people think about you has nothing to do
with you and everything to do with them.'*

—*Jen Sincero*—

Daily Queen Habits

☐ MOVEMENT   ☐ STILLNESS   ☐ KINDNESS

6am ....
7am ....
8am ....
9am ....
10am ....
11am ....
12pm ....

1pm ....
2pm ....
3pm ....
4pm ....
5pm ....
6pm ....
7pm ....

....
....
....
....
....
....
....
....
....
....
....
....
....

Take three long deep breaths and smile.

Date: /   /   Time I woke up:

How would you rate your mood this morning? 0 1 2 3 4 5 6 7 8 9 10

Choose three power affirmations to raise your vibration:

👑 ....

👑 ....

👑 ....

Your Inner Queen always has a message for you.
Which words of encouragement does she need you to hear today?

👑 ....

....

The world is a beautiful place. List three reasons to be grateful today:

👑 ....

👑 ....

👑 ....

Choose three inspired actions to make today amazing:

👑 ....

👑 ....

👑 ....

If something tries to trip you up today, how will your Inner Queen handle it?

👑 ....

....

How will you celebrate yourself today?

👑 ....

Evening Reflection

How would you rate your mood this evening? 0 1 2 3 4 5 6 7 8 9 10

Today's big win: ....

Today's big lesson: ....

*'Make the most of yourself by fanning the tiny,
inner sparks of possibility into flames of achievement.'*

—*Golda Meir*—

Daily Queen Habits

☐ MOVEMENT   ☐ STILLNESS   ☐ KINDNESS

6am ....   1pm ....

7am ....   2pm ....

8am ....   3pm ....

9am ....   4pm ....

10am ....   5pm ....

11am ....   6pm ....

12pm ....   7pm ....

....

....

....

....

....

....

....

....

....

....

....

Take three long deep breaths and smile.

Date: /   /   Time I woke up:

How would you rate your mood this morning? 0 1 2 3 4 5 6 7 8 9 10

Choose three power affirmations to raise your vibration:

♔ ....

♔ ....

♔ ....

Your Inner Queen always has a message for you.
Which words of encouragement does she need you to hear today?

♔ ....

....

The world is a beautiful place. List three reasons to be grateful today:

♔ ....

♔ ....

♔ ....

Choose three inspired actions to make today amazing:

♔ ....

♔ ....

♔ ....

If something tries to trip you up today, how will your Inner Queen handle it?

♔ ....

....

How will you celebrate yourself today?

♔ ....

Evening Reflection

How would you rate your mood this evening? 0 1 2 3 4 5 6 7 8 9 10

Today's big win: ....

Today's big lesson: ....

57

'Power is not given to you, you have to take it.'

—Beyonce—

Daily Queen Habits

☐ MOVEMENT   ☐ STILLNESS   ☐ KINDNESS

6am ....   1pm ....

7am ....   2pm ....

8am ....   3pm ....

9am ....   4pm ....

10am ....   5pm ....

11am ....   6pm ....

12pm ....   7pm ....

....

....

....

....

....

....

....

....

....

....

....

....

....

Take three long deep breaths and smile.

Date: /   /   Time I woke up:

How would you rate your mood this morning? 0 1 2 3 4 5 6 7 8 9 10

Choose three power affirmations to raise your vibration:

👑 ....

👑 ....

👑 ....

Your Inner Queen always has a message for you.
Which words of encouragement does she need you to hear today?

👑 ....

....

The world is a beautiful place. List three reasons to be grateful today:

👑 ....

👑 ....

👑 ....

Choose three inspired actions to make today amazing:

👑 ....

👑 ....

👑 ....

If something tries to trip you up today, how will your Inner Queen handle it?

👑 ....

....

How will you celebrate yourself today?

👑 ....

Evening Reflection

How would you rate your mood this evening? 0 1 2 3 4 5 6 7 8 9 10

Today's big win: ....

Today's big lesson: ....

'You can waste time drawing lines or live your life crossing them.'

—Shonda Rhimes—

Daily Queen Habits

☐ MOVEMENT   ☐ STILLNESS   ☐ KINDNESS

6am	1pm ....
7am	2pm ....
8am	3pm ....
9am	4pm ....
10am	5pm ....
11am	6pm ....
12pm	7pm ....

....

....

....

....

....

....

....

....

....

....

....

....

....

Take three long deep breaths and smile.

Date: /   /   Time I woke up:

How would you rate your mood this morning? 0 1 2 3 4 5 6 7 8 9 10

Choose three power affirmations to raise your vibration:

♛ ....

♛ ....

♛ ....

Your Inner Queen always has a message for you.
Which words of encouragement does she need you to hear today?

♛ ....

....

The world is a beautiful place. List three reasons to be grateful today:

♛ ....

♛ ....

♛ ....

Choose three inspired actions to make today amazing:

♛ ....

♛ ....

♛ ....

If something tries to trip you up today, how will your Inner Queen handle it?

♛ ....

....

How will you celebrate yourself today?

♛ ....

Evening Reflection

How would you rate your mood this evening? 0 1 2 3 4 5 6 7 8 9 10

Today's big win: ....

Today's big lesson: ....

'If you don't risk anything, you risk even more'

—Erica Jong—

Daily Queen Habits

☐ MOVEMENT ☐ STILLNESS ☐ KINDNESS

6am .... 1pm ....

7am .... 2pm ....

8am .... 3pm ....

9am .... 4pm ....

10am .... 5pm ....

11am .... 6pm ....

12pm .... 7pm ....

....

....

....

....

....

....

....

....

....

....

....

....

....

Take three long deep breaths and smile.

Date: /   /   Time I woke up:

How would you rate your mood this morning? 0 1 2 3 4 5 6 7 8 9 10

Choose three power affirmations to raise your vibration:

👑 ....

👑 ....

👑 ....

Your Inner Queen always has a message for you.
Which words of encouragement does she need you to hear today?

👑 ....

....

The world is a beautiful place. List three reasons to be grateful today:

👑 ....

👑 ....

👑 ....

Choose three inspired actions to make today amazing:

👑 ....

👑 ....

👑 ....

If something tries to trip you up today, how will your Inner Queen handle it?

👑 ....

....

How will you celebrate yourself today?

👑 ....

Evening Reflection

How would you rate your mood this evening? 0 1 2 3 4 5 6 7 8 9 10

Today's big win: ....

Today's big lesson: ....

'Done is better than perfect.'

—Sheryl Sandberg—

Daily Queen Habits

☐ MOVEMENT   ☐ STILLNESS   ☐ KINDNESS

6am .... 1pm ....

7am .... 2pm ....

8am .... 3pm ....

9am .... 4pm ....

10am .... 5pm ....

11am .... 6pm ....

12pm .... 7pm ....

....

....

....

....

....

....

....

....

....

....

....

....

....

Take three long deep breaths and smile.

Date: /   /   Time I woke up:

How would you rate your mood this morning? 0 1 2 3 4 5 6 7 8 9 10

Choose three power affirmations to raise your vibration:

♛ ....

♛ ....

♛ ....

Your Inner Queen always has a message for you.
Which words of encouragement does she need you to hear today?

♛ ....

....

The world is a beautiful place. List three reasons to be grateful today:

♛ ....

♛ ....

♛ ....

Choose three inspired actions to make today amazing:

♛ ....

♛ ....

♛ ....

If something tries to trip you up today, how will your Inner Queen handle it?

♛ ....

....

How will you celebrate yourself today?

♛ ....

Evening Reflection

How would you rate your mood this evening? 0 1 2 3 4 5 6 7 8 9 10

Today's big win: ....

Today's big lesson: ....

'If you don't like the road you're walking, start paving another one.'

—Dolly Parton—

Daily Queen Habits

☐ MOVEMENT   ☐ STILLNESS   ☐ KINDNESS

6am .... 1pm ....

7am .... 2pm ....

8am .... 3pm ....

9am .... 4pm ....

10am .... 5pm ....

11am .... 6pm ....

12pm .... 7pm ....

....

....

....

....

....

....

....

....

....

....

....

....

....

Take three long deep breaths and smile.

Date: /   /   Time I woke up:

How would you rate your mood this morning? 0 1 2 3 4 5 6 7 8 9 10

Choose three power affirmations to raise your vibration:

♕ ....

♕ ....

♕ ....

Your Inner Queen always has a message for you.
Which words of encouragement does she need you to hear today?

♕ ....

....

The world is a beautiful place. List three reasons to be grateful today:

♕ ....

♕ ....

♕ ....

Choose three inspired actions to make today amazing:

♕ ....

♕ ....

♕ ....

If something tries to trip you up today, how will your Inner Queen handle it?

♕ ....

....

How will you celebrate yourself today?

♕ ....

Evening Reflection

How would you rate your mood this evening? 0 1 2 3 4 5 6 7 8 9 10

Today's big win: ....

Today's big lesson: ....

'You can never leave footprints that last if you are always walking on tiptoe.'

—Leymah Gbowee—

Daily Queen Habits

☐ MOVEMENT ☐ STILLNESS ☐ KINDNESS

6am .... 1pm ....

7am .... 2pm ....

8am .... 3pm ....

9am .... 4pm ....

10am .... 5pm ....

11am .... 6pm ....

12pm .... 7pm ....

....

....

....

....

....

....

....

....

....

....

....

....

Take three long deep breaths and smile.

Date: /   /   Time I woke up:

How would you rate your mood this morning? 0 1 2 3 4 5 6 7 8 9 10

Choose three power affirmations to raise your vibration:

👑 ....

👑 ....

👑 ....

Your Inner Queen always has a message for you.
Which words of encouragement does she need you to hear today?

👑 ....

....

The world is a beautiful place. List three reasons to be grateful today:

👑 ....

👑 ....

👑 ....

Choose three inspired actions to make today amazing:

👑 ....

👑 ....

👑 ....

If something tries to trip you up today, how will your Inner Queen handle it?

👑 ....

....

How will you celebrate yourself today?

👑 ....

Evening Reflection

How would you rate your mood this evening? 0 1 2 3 4 5 6 7 8 9 10

Today's big win: ....

Today's big lesson: ....

'I choose to make the rest of my life the best of my life.'
—Louise Hay—

Daily Queen Habits

☐ MOVEMENT   ☐ STILLNESS   ☐ KINDNESS

6am ....   1pm ....

7am ....   2pm ....

8am ....   3pm ....

9am ....   4pm ....

10am ....   5pm ....

11am ....   6pm ....

12pm ....   7pm ....

....

....

....

....

....

....

....

....

....

....

....

....

....

Take three long deep breaths and smile.

Date: /   /   Time I woke up:

How would you rate your mood this morning? 0 1 2 3 4 5 6 7 8 9 10

Choose three power affirmations to raise your vibration:

♔ ....

♔ ....

♔ ....

Your Inner Queen always has a message for you.
Which words of encouragement does she need you to hear today?

♔ ....

....

The world is a beautiful place. List three reasons to be grateful today:

♔ ....

♔ ....

♔ ....

Choose three inspired actions to make today amazing:

♔ ....

♔ ....

♔ ....

If something tries to trip you up today, how will your Inner Queen handle it?

♔ ....

....

How will you celebrate yourself today?

♔ ....

Evening Reflection

How would you rate your mood this evening? 0 1 2 3 4 5 6 7 8 9 10

Today's big win: ....

Today's big lesson: ....

'What you do makes a difference, and you have to decide what kind of difference you want to make.'

—*Jane Goodall*—

Daily Queen Habits

☐ MOVEMENT   ☐ STILLNESS   ☐ KINDNESS

6am ....   1pm ....

7am ....   2pm ....

8am ....   3pm ....

9am ....   4pm ....

10am ....   5pm ....

11am ....   6pm ....

12pm ....   7pm ....

....

....

....

....

....

....

....

....

....

....

....

....

Take three long deep breaths and smile.

Date: /   /   Time I woke up:

How would you rate your mood this morning? 0 1 2 3 4 5 6 7 8 9 10

Choose three power affirmations to raise your vibration:

👑 ....

👑 ....

👑 ....

Your Inner Queen always has a message for you.
Which words of encouragement does she need you to hear today?

👑 ....

....

The world is a beautiful place. List three reasons to be grateful today:

👑 ....

👑 ....

👑 ....

Choose three inspired actions to make today amazing:

👑 ....

👑 ....

👑 ....

If something tries to trip you up today, how will your Inner Queen handle it?

👑 ....

....

How will you celebrate yourself today?

👑 ....

Evening Reflection

How would you rate your mood this evening? 0 1 2 3 4 5 6 7 8 9 10

Today's big win: ....

Today's big lesson: ....

'Step out of the history that is holding you back.
Step into the new story you are willing to create.'

—Oprah—

Daily Queen Habits

☐ MOVEMENT   ☐ STILLNESS   ☐ KINDNESS

6am .... 1pm ....

7am .... 2pm ....

8am .... 3pm ....

9am .... 4pm ....

10am .... 5pm ....

11am .... 6pm ....

12pm .... 7pm ....

....

....

....

....

....

....

....

....

....

....

....

....

Take three long deep breaths and smile.

Date: /   /   Time I woke up:

How would you rate your mood this morning? 0 1 2 3 4 5 6 7 8 9 10

Choose three power affirmations to raise your vibration:

♕ ....

♕ ....

♕ ....

Your Inner Queen always has a message for you.
Which words of encouragement does she need you to hear today?

♕ ....

....

The world is a beautiful place. List three reasons to be grateful today:

♕ ....

♕ ....

♕ ....

Choose three inspired actions to make today amazing:

♕ ....

♕ ....

♕ ....

If something tries to trip you up today, how will your Inner Queen handle it?

♕ ....

....

How will you celebrate yourself today?

♕ ....

Evening Reflection

How would you rate your mood this evening? 0 1 2 3 4 5 6 7 8 9 10

Today's big win: ....

Today's big lesson: ....

*'What lies behind you and what lies in front of you, pales
in comparison to what lies inside of you.'*

Daily Queen Habits

☐ MOVEMENT   ☐ STILLNESS   ☐ KINDNESS

6am .... 1pm ....

7am .... 2pm ....

8am .... 3pm ....

9am .... 4pm ....

10am .... 5pm ....

11am .... 6pm ....

12pm .... 7pm ....

....

....

....

....

....

....

....

....

....

....

....

....

30 Day Reflections

Looking back over the last month, what has changed for you?

....

....

....

....

....

....

My Biggest Win ....

....

My Biggest Lesson ....

....

Rate your overall commitment to this journal .... %

Which habit/s have you found easiest to build?

....

Which habit/s have you had most resistance to?

....

What are your goals for the next 30 days?

1. ....

2. ....

3. ....

Life Assessment

Rate where you feel you are in each area right now
(1 being low vibration and 10 being high vibe!)

Energy   1   2   3   4   5   6   7   8   9   10

I feel energised, healthy and I'm moving my body regularly.

Mental Health   1   2   3   4   5   6   7   8   9   10

I am compassionate towards myself and have a kind, uplifting inner dialogue.

Relationships/Love   1   2   3   4   5   6   7   8   9   10

I have a deep, meaningful and healthy connection with my partner. My relationship brings me joy and fulfilment. (If single: I have a deep, meaningful and healthy connection with myself. I nurture myself and show myself love.)

Purpose   1   2   3   4   5   6   7   8   9   10

I am finding my purpose in this world. I am committed to feeling fulfilled and excited by my life. I follow my heart and listen to my inner guidance.

Circle   1   2   3   4   5   6   7   8   9   10

I am surrounded by uplifting, supportive people who raise me higher and inspire me to be the best version of myself.

Self Care   1   2   3   4   5   6   7   8   9   10

I spend time taking care of myself, allowing myself to rest and recover and treat myself with loving kindness.

Connection   1   2   3   4   5   6   7   8   9   10

I feel a deep sense of connection to my Inner Queen. I understand that I am always being supported by the Universe and can ask for help and guidance whenever I need it.

Abundance   1   2   3   4   5   6   7   8   9   10

I see abundance all around me and understand that the Universe is overflowing with everything I could ever need to thrive. I am generous because I know that there is always enough to go around. I am open to receiving all of the goodness life has to offer.

Growth   1   2   3   4   5   6   7   8   9   10

I have the courage to try new things and pursue my dreams everyday. I use adversity to learn, grow and adapt, and I understand that growth is an integral part of my journey.

Take a moment to pause
and really celebrate how far you have come.

Take three long deep breaths and smile.

Date: /   /   Time I woke up:

How would you rate your mood this morning? 0 1 2 3 4 5 6 7 8 9 10

Choose three power affirmations to raise your vibration:

....

....

....

Your Inner Queen always has a message for you.
Which words of encouragement does she need you to hear today?

....

....

The world is a beautiful place. List three reasons to be grateful today:

....

....

....

Choose three inspired actions to make today amazing:

....

....

....

If something tries to trip you up today, how will your Inner Queen handle it?

....

....

How will you celebrate yourself today?

....

Evening Reflection

How would you rate your mood this evening? 0 1 2 3 4 5 6 7 8 9 10

Today's big win: ....

Today's big lesson: ....

Daily Queen Habits

☐ MOVEMENT ☐ STILLNESS ☐ KINDNESS

6am .... 1pm ....

7am .... 2pm ....

8am .... 3pm ....

9am .... 4pm ....

10am .... 5pm ....

11am .... 6pm ....

12pm .... 7pm ....

....

....

....

....

....

....

....

....

....

....

....

Take three long deep breaths and smile.

Date: /   /   Time I woke up:

How would you rate your mood this morning? 0 1 2 3 4 5 6 7 8 9 10

Choose three power affirmations to raise your vibration:

♔ ....

♔ ....

♔ ....

Your Inner Queen always has a message for you.
Which words of encouragement does she need you to hear today?

♔ ....

....

The world is a beautiful place. List three reasons to be grateful today:

♔ ....

♔ ....

♔ ....

Choose three inspired actions to make today amazing:

♔ ....

♔ ....

♔ ....

If something tries to trip you up today, how will your Inner Queen handle it?

♔ ....

....

How will you celebrate yourself today?

♔ ....

Evening Reflection

How would you rate your mood this evening? 0 1 2 3 4 5 6 7 8 9 10

Today's big win: ....

Today's big lesson: ....

'There is no greater agony than bearing an untold story inside you.'

—Maya Angelo—

Daily Queen Habits

☐ MOVEMENT   ☐ STILLNESS   ☐ KINDNESS

6am ....   1pm ....

7am ....   2pm ....

8am ....   3pm ....

9am ....   4pm ....

10am ....   5pm ....

11am ....   6pm ....

12pm ....   7pm ....

....

....

....

....

....

....

....

....

....

....

....

....

....

Take three long deep breaths and smile.

Date: /   /   Time I woke up:

How would you rate your mood this morning? 0 1 2 3 4 5 6 7 8 9 10

Choose three power affirmations to raise your vibration:

♛ ....

♛ ....

♛ ....

Your Inner Queen always has a message for you.
Which words of encouragement does she need you to hear today?

♛ ....

....

The world is a beautiful place. List three reasons to be grateful today:

♛ ....

♛ ....

♛ ....

Choose three inspired actions to make today amazing:

♛ ....

♛ ....

♛ ....

If something tries to trip you up today, how will your Inner Queen handle it?

♛ ....

....

How will you celebrate yourself today?

♛ ....

Evening Reflection

How would you rate your mood this evening? 0 1 2 3 4 5 6 7 8 9 10

Today's big win: ....

Today's big lesson: ....

'If you change the way you look at things, the things you look at change.'

—Wayne Dyer—

Daily Queen Habits

☐ MOVEMENT   ☐ STILLNESS   ☐ KINDNESS

6am ....   1pm ....

7am ....   2pm ....

8am ....   3pm ....

9am ....   4pm ....

10am ....   5pm ....

11am ....   6pm ....

12pm ....   7pm ....

....

....

....

....

....

....

....

....

....

....

....

....

....

Take three long deep breaths and smile.

Date: /   /   Time I woke up:

How would you rate your mood this morning? 0 1 2 3 4 5 6 7 8 9 10

Choose three power affirmations to raise your vibration:

♛ ....

♛ ....

♛ ....

Your Inner Queen always has a message for you.
Which words of encouragement does she need you to hear today?

♛ ....

....

The world is a beautiful place. List three reasons to be grateful today:

♛ ....

♛ ....

♛ ....

Choose three inspired actions to make today amazing:

♛ ....

♛ ....

♛ ....

If something tries to trip you up today, how will your Inner Queen handle it?

♛ ....

....

How will you celebrate yourself today?

♛ ....

Evening Reflection

How would you rate your mood this evening? 0 1 2 3 4 5 6 7 8 9 10

Today's big win: ....

Today's big lesson: ....

'Spread love everywhere you go.'

—*Mother Teresa*—

Daily Queen Habits

☐ MOVEMENT   ☐ STILLNESS   ☐ KINDNESS

6am .... 1pm ....

7am .... 2pm ....

8am .... 3pm ....

9am .... 4pm ....

10am .... 5pm ....

11am .... 6pm ....

12pm .... 7pm ....

....

....

....

....

....

....

....

....

....

....

....

....

....

Take three long deep breaths and smile.

Date: /   /   Time I woke up:

How would you rate your mood this morning? 0 1 2 3 4 5 6 7 8 9 10

Choose three power affirmations to raise your vibration:

👑 ....

👑 ....

👑 ....

Your Inner Queen always has a message for you.
Which words of encouragement does she need you to hear today?

👑 ....

....

The world is a beautiful place. List three reasons to be grateful today:

👑 ....

👑 ....

👑 ....

Choose three inspired actions to make today amazing:

👑 ....

👑 ....

👑 ....

If something tries to trip you up today, how will your Inner Queen handle it?

👑 ....

....

How will you celebrate yourself today?

👑 ....

Evening Reflection

How would you rate your mood this evening? 0 1 2 3 4 5 6 7 8 9 10

Today's big win: ....

Today's big lesson: ....

'Above all, be the heroine of your life, not the victim.'

—Nora Ephron—

Daily Queen Habits

☐ MOVEMENT　　　　　☐ STILLNESS　　　　　☐ KINDNESS

6am ....　1pm ....

7am ....　2pm ....

8am ....　3pm ....

9am ....　4pm ....

10am ....　5pm ....

11am ....　6pm ....

12pm ....　7pm ....

....

....

....

....

....

....

....

....

....

....

....

....

....

Take three long deep breaths and smile.

Date: /   /   Time I woke up:

How would you rate your mood this morning? 0 1 2 3 4 5 6 7 8 9 10

Choose three power affirmations to raise your vibration:

♛ ....

♛ ....

♛ ....

Your Inner Queen always has a message for you.
Which words of encouragement does she need you to hear today?

♛ ....

....

The world is a beautiful place. List three reasons to be grateful today:

♛ ....

♛ ....

♛ ....

Choose three inspired actions to make today amazing:

♛ ....

♛ ....

♛ ....

If something tries to trip you up today, how will your Inner Queen handle it?

♛ ....

....

How will you celebrate yourself today?

♛ ....

Evening Reflection

How would you rate your mood this evening? 0 1 2 3 4 5 6 7 8 9 10

Today's big win: ....

Today's big lesson: ....

'Doubt is a killer. You just have to know who you are and what you stand for.'

—Jennifer Lopez—

Daily Queen Habits

☐ MOVEMENT ☐ STILLNESS ☐ KINDNESS

6am	....	1pm	....
7am	....	2pm	....
8am	....	3pm	....
9am	....	4pm	....
10am	....	5pm	....
11am	....	6pm	....
12pm	....	7pm	....

....

....

....

....

....

....

....

....

....

....

....

....

....

Take three long deep breaths and smile.

Date: /   /   Time I woke up:

How would you rate your mood this morning? 0 1 2 3 4 5 6 7 8 9 10

Choose three power affirmations to raise your vibration:

👑 ....

👑 ....

👑 ....

Your Inner Queen always has a message for you.
Which words of encouragement does she need you to hear today?

👑 ....

....

The world is a beautiful place. List three reasons to be grateful today:

👑 ....

👑 ....

👑 ....

Choose three inspired actions to make today amazing:

👑 ....

👑 ....

👑 ....

If something tries to trip you up today, how will your Inner Queen handle it?

👑 ....

....

How will you celebrate yourself today?

👑 ....

Evening Reflection

How would you rate your mood this evening? 0 1 2 3 4 5 6 7 8 9 10

Today's big win: ....

Today's big lesson: ....

'I'm always perpetually out of my comfort zone'

—Tory Burch—

Daily Queen Habits

☐ MOVEMENT   ☐ STILLNESS   ☐ KINDNESS

6am ....   1pm ....

7am ....   2pm ....

8am ....   3pm ....

9am ....   4pm ....

10am ....   5pm ....

11am ....   6pm ....

12pm ....   7pm ....

....

....

....

....

....

....

....

....

....

....

....

....

....

....

Take three long deep breaths and smile.

Date: /   /   Time I woke up:

How would you rate your mood this morning? 0 1 2 3 4 5 6 7 8 9 10

Choose three power affirmations to raise your vibration:

♕ ....

♕ ....

♕ ....

Your Inner Queen always has a message for you.
Which words of encouragement does she need you to hear today?

♕ ....

....

The world is a beautiful place. List three reasons to be grateful today:

♕ ....

♕ ....

♕ ....

Choose three inspired actions to make today amazing:

♕ ....

♕ ....

♕ ....

If something tries to trip you up today, how will your Inner Queen handle it?

♕ ....

....

How will you celebrate yourself today?

♕ ....

Evening Reflection

How would you rate your mood this evening? 0 1 2 3 4 5 6 7 8 9 10

Today's big win: ....

Today's big lesson: ....

*'Owning our story can be hard but not nearly as difficult
as spending our lives running from it.'*

—*Brene Brown*—

Daily Queen Habits

☐ MOVEMENT   ☐ STILLNESS   ☐ KINDNESS

6am ....   1pm ....

7am ....   2pm ....

8am ....   3pm ....

9am ....   4pm ....

10am ....   5pm ....

11am ....   6pm ....

12pm ....   7pm ....

....

....

....

....

....

....

....

....

....

....

....

....

Take three long deep breaths and smile.

Date: /   /   Time I woke up:

How would you rate your mood this morning? 0 1 2 3 4 5 6 7 8 9 10

Choose three power affirmations to raise your vibration:

♛ ....

♛ ....

♛ ....

Your Inner Queen always has a message for you.
Which words of encouragement does she need you to hear today?

♛ ....

....

The world is a beautiful place. List three reasons to be grateful today:

♛ ....

♛ ....

♛ ....

Choose three inspired actions to make today amazing:

♛ ....

♛ ....

♛ ....

If something tries to trip you up today, how will your Inner Queen handle it?

♛ ....

....

How will you celebrate yourself today?

♛ ....

Evening Reflection

How would you rate your mood this evening? 0 1 2 3 4 5 6 7 8 9 10

Today's big win: ....

Today's big lesson: ....

'Get to know yourself and show up as her. Fully, boldly, completely, unapologetically.'

—Megan Rose Lane—

Daily Queen Habits

☐ MOVEMENT   ☐ STILLNESS   ☐ KINDNESS

6am ....   1pm ....

7am ....   2pm ....

8am ....   3pm ....

9am ....   4pm ....

10am ....   5pm ....

11am ....   6pm ....

12pm ....   7pm ....

....

....

....

....

....

....

....

....

....

....

....

....

....

Take three long deep breaths and smile.

Date: /   /   Time I woke up:

How would you rate your mood this morning? 0 1 2 3 4 5 6 7 8 9 10

Choose three power affirmations to raise your vibration:

♛ ....

♛ ....

♛ ....

Your Inner Queen always has a message for you.
Which words of encouragement does she need you to hear today?

♛ ....

....

The world is a beautiful place. List three reasons to be grateful today:

♛ ....

♛ ....

♛ ....

Choose three inspired actions to make today amazing:

♛ ....

♛ ....

♛ ....

If something tries to trip you up today, how will your Inner Queen handle it?

♛ ....

....

How will you celebrate yourself today?

♛ ....

Evening Reflection

How would you rate your mood this evening? 0 1 2 3 4 5 6 7 8 9 10

Today's big win: ....

Today's big lesson: ....

'Start before you are ready and start with conviction for change.'

—The Completion Coach—

Daily Queen Habits

☐ MOVEMENT   ☐ STILLNESS   ☐ KINDNESS

6am ....   1pm ....

7am ....   2pm ....

8am ....   3pm ....

9am ....   4pm ....

10am ....   5pm ....

11am ....   6pm ....

12pm ....   7pm ....

....

....

....

....

....

....

....

....

....

....

....

....

....

Take three long deep breaths and smile.

Date: /   /   Time I woke up:

How would you rate your mood this morning? 0 1 2 3 4 5 6 7 8 9 10

Choose three power affirmations to raise your vibration:

♛ ....

♛ ....

♛ ....

Your Inner Queen always has a message for you.
Which words of encouragement does she need you to hear today?

♛ ....

....

The world is a beautiful place. List three reasons to be grateful today:

♛ ....

♛ ....

♛ ....

Choose three inspired actions to make today amazing:

♛ ....

♛ ....

♛ ....

If something tries to trip you up today, how will your Inner Queen handle it?

♛ ....

....

How will you celebrate yourself today?

♛ ....

Evening Reflection

How would you rate your mood this evening? 0 1 2 3 4 5 6 7 8 9 10

Today's big win: ....

Today's big lesson: ....

'Your thoughts are incredibly powerful. Choose yours wisely.'

—*Joe Dispenza*—

Daily Queen Habits

☐ MOVEMENT   ☐ STILLNESS   ☐ KINDNESS

6am	....	1pm	....
7am	....	2pm	....
8am	....	3pm	....
9am	....	4pm	....
10am	....	5pm	....
11am	....	6pm	....
12pm	....	7pm	....

....

....

....

....

....

....

....

....

....

....

....

....

Take three long deep breaths and smile.

Date: /   /   Time I woke up:

How would you rate your mood this morning? 0 1 2 3 4 5 6 7 8 9 10

Choose three power affirmations to raise your vibration:

♛ ....

♛ ....

♛ ....

Your Inner Queen always has a message for you.
Which words of encouragement does she need you to hear today?

♛ ....

....

The world is a beautiful place. List three reasons to be grateful today:

♛ ....

♛ ....

♛ ....

Choose three inspired actions to make today amazing:

♛ ....

♛ ....

♛ ....

If something tries to trip you up today, how will your Inner Queen handle it?

♛ ....

....

How will you celebrate yourself today?

♛ ....

Evening Reflection

How would you rate your mood this evening? 0 1 2 3 4 5 6 7 8 9 10

Today's big win: ....

Today's big lesson: ....

103

Daily Queen Habits

☐ MOVEMENT   ☐ STILLNESS   ☐ KINDNESS

6am	....	1pm	....
7am	....	2pm	....
8am	....	3pm	....
9am	....	4pm	....
10am	....	5pm	....
11am	....	6pm	....
12pm	....	7pm	....

Take three long deep breaths and smile.

Date: /   /   Time I woke up:

How would you rate your mood this morning? 0 1 2 3 4 5 6 7 8 9 10

Choose three power affirmations to raise your vibration:

♛ ....

♛ ....

♛ ....

Your Inner Queen always has a message for you.
Which words of encouragement does she need you to hear today?

♛ ....

....

The world is a beautiful place. List three reasons to be grateful today:

♛ ....

♛ ....

♛ ....

Choose three inspired actions to make today amazing:

♛ ....

♛ ....

♛ ....

If something tries to trip you up today, how will your Inner Queen handle it?

♛ ....

....

How will you celebrate yourself today?

♛ ....

Evening Reflection

How would you rate your mood this evening? 0 1 2 3 4 5 6 7 8 9 10

Today's big win: ....

Today's big lesson: ....

'I always did something I was a little not ready to do. I think that's how you grow.'

—Marissa Mayer—

Daily Queen Habits

☐ MOVEMENT   ☐ STILLNESS   ☐ KINDNESS

6am ....   1pm ....

7am ....   2pm ....

8am ....   3pm ....

9am ....   4pm ....

10am ....   5pm ....

11am ....   6pm ....

12pm ....   7pm ....

....

....

....

....

....

....

....

....

....

....

....

....

....

Take three long deep breaths and smile.

Date: /   /   Time I woke up:

How would you rate your mood this morning? 0 1 2 3 4 5 6 7 8 9 10

Choose three power affirmations to raise your vibration:

👑 ....

👑 ....

👑 ....

Your Inner Queen always has a message for you.
Which words of encouragement does she need you to hear today?

👑 ....

....

The world is a beautiful place. List three reasons to be grateful today:

👑 ....

👑 ....

👑 ....

Choose three inspired actions to make today amazing:

👑 ....

👑 ....

👑 ....

If something tries to trip you up today, how will your Inner Queen handle it?

👑 ....

....

How will you celebrate yourself today?

👑 ....

Evening Reflection

How would you rate your mood this evening? 0 1 2 3 4 5 6 7 8 9 10

Today's big win: ....

Today's big lesson: ....

'Think like a queen. A queen is not afraid to fail.
Failure is another stepping stone to greatness.'

—Oprah Winfrey—

Daily Queen Habits

☐ MOVEMENT   ☐ STILLNESS   ☐ KINDNESS

6am .... 1pm ....

7am .... 2pm ....

8am .... 3pm ....

9am .... 4pm ....

10am .... 5pm ....

11am .... 6pm ....

12pm .... 7pm ....

....

....

....

....

....

....

....

....

....

....

....

Take three long deep breaths and smile.

Date: /   /   Time I woke up:

How would you rate your mood this morning? 0 1 2 3 4 5 6 7 8 9 10

Choose three power affirmations to raise your vibration:

♔ ....

♔ ....

♔ ....

Your Inner Queen always has a message for you.
Which words of encouragement does she need you to hear today?

♔ ....

....

The world is a beautiful place. List three reasons to be grateful today:

♔ ....

♔ ....

♔ ....

Choose three inspired actions to make today amazing:

♔ ....

♔ ....

♔ ....

If something tries to trip you up today, how will your Inner Queen handle it?

♔ ....

....

How will you celebrate yourself today?

♔ ....

Evening Reflection

How would you rate your mood this evening? 0 1 2 3 4 5 6 7 8 9 10

Today's big win: ....

Today's big lesson: ....

"I found that ultimately if you truly pour your heart into what you believe in — even if it makes you vulnerable — amazing things can and will happen."

—Emma Watson—

Daily Queen Habits

☐ MOVEMENT   ☐ STILLNESS   ☐ KINDNESS

6am .... 1pm ....

7am .... 2pm ....

8am .... 3pm ....

9am .... 4pm ....

10am .... 5pm ....

11am .... 6pm ....

12pm .... 7pm ....

....

....

....

....

....

....

....

....

....

....

....

....

Take three long deep breaths and smile.

Date: /   /   Time I woke up:

How would you rate your mood this morning? 0 1 2 3 4 5 6 7 8 9 10

Choose three power affirmations to raise your vibration:

👑 ....

👑 ....

👑 ....

Your Inner Queen always has a message for you.
Which words of encouragement does she need you to hear today?

👑 ....

....

The world is a beautiful place. List three reasons to be grateful today:

👑 ....

👑 ....

👑 ....

Choose three inspired actions to make today amazing:

👑 ....

👑 ....

👑 ....

If something tries to trip you up today, how will your Inner Queen handle it?

👑 ....

....

How will you celebrate yourself today?

👑 ....

Evening Reflection

How would you rate your mood this evening? 0 1 2 3 4 5 6 7 8 9 10

Today's big win: ....

Today's big lesson: ....

'Never be ashamed of what you feel. You have the right to feel any emotion that you want, and to do what makes you happy.'

—*Demi Lovato*—

Daily Queen Habits

☐ MOVEMENT　　　　　☐ STILLNESS　　　　　☐ KINDNESS

6am ....

7am ....

8am ....

9am ....

10am ....

11am ....

12pm ....

1pm ....

2pm ....

3pm ....

4pm ....

5pm ....

6pm ....

7pm ....

....

....

....

....

....

....

....

....

....

....

....

....

Take three long deep breaths and smile.

Date: /   /   Time I woke up:

How would you rate your mood this morning? 0 1 2 3 4 5 6 7 8 9 10

Choose three power affirmations to raise your vibration:

♛ ....

♛ ....

♛ ....

Your Inner Queen always has a message for you.
Which words of encouragement does she need you to hear today?

♛ ....

....

The world is a beautiful place. List three reasons to be grateful today:

♛ ....

♛ ....

♛ ....

Choose three inspired actions to make today amazing:

♛ ....

♛ ....

♛ ....

If something tries to trip you up today, how will your Inner Queen handle it?

♛ ....

....

How will you celebrate yourself today?

♛ ....

Evening Reflection

How would you rate your mood this evening? 0 1 2 3 4 5 6 7 8 9 10

Today's big win: ....

Today's big lesson: ....

'No one can make you feel inferior without your consent.'
—Eleanor Roosevelt—

Daily Queen Habits

☐ MOVEMENT   ☐ STILLNESS   ☐ KINDNESS

6am ....   1pm ....

7am ....   2pm ....

8am ....   3pm ....

9am ....   4pm ....

10am ....   5pm ....

11am ....   6pm ....

12pm ....   7pm ....

....

....

....

....

....

....

....

....

....

....

....

....

....

Take three long deep breaths and smile.

Date: /   /   Time I woke up:

How would you rate your mood this morning? 0 1 2 3 4 5 6 7 8 9 10

Choose three power affirmations to raise your vibration:

♛ ....

♛ ....

♛ ....

Your Inner Queen always has a message for you.
Which words of encouragement does she need you to hear today?

♛ ....

....

The world is a beautiful place. List three reasons to be grateful today:

♛ ....

♛ ....

♛ ....

Choose three inspired actions to make today amazing:

♛ ....

♛ ....

♛ ....

If something tries to trip you up today, how will your Inner Queen handle it?

♛ ....

....

How will you celebrate yourself today?

♛ ....

Evening Reflection

How would you rate your mood this evening? 0 1 2 3 4 5 6 7 8 9 10

Today's big win: ....

Today's big lesson: ....

'As women, we have to start appreciating our own worth and each other's worth. Seek out strong women to befriend, to align yourself with, to learn from.'

—*Madonna*—

Daily Queen Habits

☐ MOVEMENT   ☐ STILLNESS   ☐ KINDNESS

6am ....

7am ....

8am ....

9am ....

10am ....

11am ....

12pm ....

1pm ....

2pm ....

3pm ....

4pm ....

5pm ....

6pm ....

7pm ....

....

....

....

....

....

....

....

....

....

....

....

....

Take three long deep breaths and smile.

Date: /   /   Time I woke up:

How would you rate your mood this morning? 0 1 2 3 4 5 6 7 8 9 10

Choose three power affirmations to raise your vibration:

♕ ....

♕ ....

♕ ....

Your Inner Queen always has a message for you.
Which words of encouragement does she need you to hear today?

♕ ....

....

The world is a beautiful place. List three reasons to be grateful today:

♕ ....

♕ ....

♕ ....

Choose three inspired actions to make today amazing:

♕ ....

♕ ....

♕ ....

If something tries to trip you up today, how will your Inner Queen handle it?

♕ ....

....

How will you celebrate yourself today?

♕ ....

Evening Reflection

How would you rate your mood this evening? 0 1 2 3 4 5 6 7 8 9 10

Today's big win: ....

Today's big lesson: ....

*'When I dare to be powerful, to use my strength in the service of my vision,
then it becomes less and less important whether I am afraid.'*

—Audre Lord—

Daily Queen Habits

☐ MOVEMENT   ☐ STILLNESS   ☐ KINDNESS

6am .... 1pm ....

7am .... 2pm ....

8am .... 3pm ....

9am .... 4pm ....

10am .... 5pm ....

11am .... 6pm ....

12pm .... 7pm ....

....

....

....

....

....

....

....

....

....

....

....

....

Date: /   /   Time I woke up:

How would you rate your mood this morning? 0 1 2 3 4 5 6 7 8 9 10

Choose three power affirmations to raise your vibration:

♔ ....

♔ ....

♔ ....

Your Inner Queen always has a message for you.
Which words of encouragement does she need you to hear today?

♔ ....

....

The world is a beautiful place. List three reasons to be grateful today:

♔ ....

♔ ....

♔ ....

Choose three inspired actions to make today amazing:

♔ ....

♔ ....

♔ ....

If something tries to trip you up today, how will your Inner Queen handle it?

♔ ....

....

How will you celebrate yourself today?

♔ ....

Evening Reflection

How would you rate your mood this evening? 0 1 2 3 4 5 6 7 8 9 10

Today's big win: ....

Today's big lesson: ....

*'Without leaps of imagination, or dreaming, we lose the excitement
of possibilities. Dreaming, after all, is a form of planning.'*
—Gloria Steinem—

Daily Queen Habits

☐ MOVEMENT   ☐ STILLNESS   ☐ KINDNESS

6am ....   1pm ....

7am ....   2pm ....

8am ....   3pm ....

9am ....   4pm ....

10am ....   5pm ....

11am ....   6pm ....

12pm ....   7pm ....

....

....

....

....

....

....

....

....

....

....

....

....

Take three long deep breaths and smile.

Date: /   /   Time I woke up:

How would you rate your mood this morning? 0 1 2 3 4 5 6 7 8 9 10

Choose three power affirmations to raise your vibration:

♛ ....

♛ ....

♛ ....

Your Inner Queen always has a message for you.
Which words of encouragement does she need you to hear today?

♛ ....

....

The world is a beautiful place. List three reasons to be grateful today:

♛ ....

♛ ....

♛ ....

Choose three inspired actions to make today amazing:

♛ ....

♛ ....

♛ ....

If something tries to trip you up today, how will your Inner Queen handle it?

♛ ....

....

How will you celebrate yourself today?

♛ ....

Evening Reflection

How would you rate your mood this evening? 0 1 2 3 4 5 6 7 8 9 10

Today's big win: ....

Today's big lesson: ....

121

'We cannot all succeed when half of us are held back. We call upon our sisters around the world to be brave — to embrace the strength within themselves and realize their full potential.'

—Malala Yousafzai—

Daily Queen Habits

☐ MOVEMENT   ☐ STILLNESS   ☐ KINDNESS

6am ....   1pm ....

7am ....   2pm ....

8am ....   3pm ....

9am ....   4pm ....

10am ....   5pm ....

11am ....   6pm ....

12pm ....   7pm ....

....

....

....

....

....

....

....

....

....

....

....

Take three long deep breaths and smile.

Date: /   /   Time I woke up:

How would you rate your mood this morning? 0 1 2 3 4 5 6 7 8 9 10

Choose three power affirmations to raise your vibration:

♕ ....

♕ ....

♕ ....

Your Inner Queen always has a message for you.
Which words of encouragement does she need you to hear today?

♕ ....

....

The world is a beautiful place. List three reasons to be grateful today:

♕ ....

♕ ....

♕ ....

Choose three inspired actions to make today amazing:

♕ ....

♕ ....

♕ ....

If something tries to trip you up today, how will your Inner Queen handle it?

♕ ....

....

How will you celebrate yourself today?

♕ ....

Evening Reflection

How would you rate your mood this evening? 0 1 2 3 4 5 6 7 8 9 10

Today's big win: ....

Today's big lesson: ....

'The most common way people give up their power is by thinking they don't have any.'

—Alice Walker—

Daily Queen Habits

☐ MOVEMENT   ☐ STILLNESS   ☐ KINDNESS

6am ....   1pm ....

7am ....   2pm ....

8am ....   3pm ....

9am ....   4pm ....

10am ....   5pm ....

11am ....   6pm ....

12pm ....   7pm ....

....

....

....

....

....

....

....

....

....

....

....

....

....

Take three long deep breaths and smile.

Date: /   /   Time I woke up:

How would you rate your mood this morning? 0 1 2 3 4 5 6 7 8 9 10

Choose three power affirmations to raise your vibration:

👑 ....

👑 ....

👑 ....

Your Inner Queen always has a message for you.
Which words of encouragement does she need you to hear today?

👑 ....

....

The world is a beautiful place. List three reasons to be grateful today:

👑 ....

👑 ....

👑 ....

Choose three inspired actions to make today amazing:

👑 ....

👑 ....

👑 ....

If something tries to trip you up today, how will your Inner Queen handle it?

👑 ....

....

How will you celebrate yourself today?

👑 ....

Evening Reflection

How would you rate your mood this evening? 0 1 2 3 4 5 6 7 8 9 10

Today's big win: ....

Today's big lesson: ....

'Nothing liberates our greatness like the desire to help, the desire to serve.'

—*Marianne Williamson*—

Daily Queen Habits

☐ MOVEMENT ☐ STILLNESS ☐ KINDNESS

6am .... 1pm ....

7am .... 2pm ....

8am .... 3pm ....

9am .... 4pm ....

10am .... 5pm ....

11am .... 6pm ....

12pm .... 7pm ....

....

....

....

....

....

....

....

....

....

....

....

....

....

Take three long deep breaths and smile.

Date: /   /   Time I woke up:

How would you rate your mood this morning? 0 1 2 3 4 5 6 7 8 9 10

Choose three power affirmations to raise your vibration:

♛ ....

♛ ....

♛ ....

Your Inner Queen always has a message for you.
Which words of encouragement does she need you to hear today?

♛ ....

....

The world is a beautiful place. List three reasons to be grateful today:

♛ ....

♛ ....

♛ ....

Choose three inspired actions to make today amazing:

♛ ....

♛ ....

♛ ....

If something tries to trip you up today, how will your Inner Queen handle it?

♛ ....

....

How will you celebrate yourself today?

♛ ....

Evening Reflection

How would you rate your mood this evening? 0 1 2 3 4 5 6 7 8 9 10

Today's big win: ....

Today's big lesson: ....

*'Courage doesn't always roar. Sometimes courage is the little voice
at the end of the day that says I'll try again tomorrow.'*

—*Mary Anne Radmacher*—

Daily Queen Habits

☐ MOVEMENT   ☐ STILLNESS   ☐ KINDNESS

6am ....

7am ....

8am ....

9am ....

10am ....

11am ....

12pm ....

1pm ....

2pm ....

3pm ....

4pm ....

5pm ....

6pm ....

7pm ....

....

....

....

....

....

....

....

....

....

....

....

Take three long deep breaths and smile.

Date: /   /   Time I woke up:

How would you rate your mood this morning? 0 1 2 3 4 5 6 7 8 9 10

Choose three power affirmations to raise your vibration:

👑 ....

👑 ....

👑 ....

Your Inner Queen always has a message for you.
Which words of encouragement does she need you to hear today?

👑 ....

....

The world is a beautiful place. List three reasons to be grateful today:

👑 ....

👑 ....

👑 ....

Choose three inspired actions to make today amazing:

👑 ....

👑 ....

👑 ....

If something tries to trip you up today, how will your Inner Queen handle it?

👑 ....

....

How will you celebrate yourself today?

👑 ....

Evening Reflection

How would you rate your mood this evening? 0 1 2 3 4 5 6 7 8 9 10

Today's big win: ....

Today's big lesson: ....

'I've never seen any life transformation that didn't begin with the person in question finally getting tired of their own bullshit.'

—Elizabeth Gilbert—

Daily Queen Habits

☐ MOVEMENT   ☐ STILLNESS   ☐ KINDNESS

6am ....   1pm ....

7am ....   2pm ....

8am ....   3pm ....

9am ....   4pm ....

10am ....   5pm ....

11am ....   6pm ....

12pm ....   7pm ....

....

....

....

....

....

....

....

....

....

....

....

....

Take three long deep breaths and smile.

Date: /   /   Time I woke up:

How would you rate your mood this morning? 0 1 2 3 4 5 6 7 8 9 10

Choose three power affirmations to raise your vibration:

👑 ....

👑 ....

👑 ....

Your Inner Queen always has a message for you.
Which words of encouragement does she need you to hear today?

👑 ....

....

The world is a beautiful place. List three reasons to be grateful today:

👑 ....

👑 ....

👑 ....

Choose three inspired actions to make today amazing:

👑 ....

👑 ....

👑 ....

If something tries to trip you up today, how will your Inner Queen handle it?

👑 ....

....

How will you celebrate yourself today?

👑 ....

Evening Reflection

How would you rate your mood this evening? 0 1 2 3 4 5 6 7 8 9 10

Today's big win: ....

Today's big lesson: ....

'Conscious thoughts, repeated often enough, become unconscious thinking.'

—*Joe Dispenza*—

Daily Queen Habits

☐ MOVEMENT   ☐ STILLNESS   ☐ KINDNESS

6am	1pm	
7am	2pm	
8am	3pm	
9am	4pm	
10am	5pm	
11am	6pm	
12pm	7pm	

....

....

....

....

....

....

....

....

....

....

....

....

....

....

Take three long deep breaths and smile.

Date: /   /   Time I woke up:

How would you rate your mood this morning? 0 1 2 3 4 5 6 7 8 9 10

Choose three power affirmations to raise your vibration:

♛ ....

♛ ....

♛ ....

Your Inner Queen always has a message for you.
Which words of encouragement does she need you to hear today?

♛ ....

....

The world is a beautiful place. List three reasons to be grateful today:

♛ ....

♛ ....

♛ ....

Choose three inspired actions to make today amazing:

♛ ....

♛ ....

♛ ....

If something tries to trip you up today, how will your Inner Queen handle it?

♛ ....

....

How will you celebrate yourself today?

♛ ....

Evening Reflection

How would you rate your mood this evening? 0 1 2 3 4 5 6 7 8 9 10

Today's big win: ....

Today's big lesson: ....

'I can't be everything to everyone else if I am nothing to myself'

—Alex Elle—

Daily Queen Habits

☐ MOVEMENT   ☐ STILLNESS   ☐ KINDNESS

6am ....   1pm ....

7am ....   2pm ....

8am ....   3pm ....

9am ....   4pm ....

10am ....   5pm ....

11am ....   6pm ....

12pm ....   7pm ....

....

....

....

....

....

....

....

....

....

....

....

....

....

Take three long deep breaths and smile.

Date: /   /   Time I woke up:

How would you rate your mood this morning? 0 1 2 3 4 5 6 7 8 9 10

Choose three power affirmations to raise your vibration:

👑 ....

👑 ....

👑 ....

Your Inner Queen always has a message for you.
Which words of encouragement does she need you to hear today?

👑 ....

....

The world is a beautiful place. List three reasons to be grateful today:

👑 ....

👑 ....

👑 ....

Choose three inspired actions to make today amazing:

👑 ....

👑 ....

👑 ....

If something tries to trip you up today, how will your Inner Queen handle it?

👑 ....

....

How will you celebrate yourself today?

👑 ....

Evening Reflection

How would you rate your mood this evening? 0 1 2 3 4 5 6 7 8 9 10

Today's big win: ....

Today's big lesson: ....

'I am worthy and deserving of the best the world has to offer.'

Daily Queen Habits

☐ MOVEMENT   ☐ STILLNESS   ☐ KINDNESS

6am .... 1pm ....

7am .... 2pm ....

8am .... 3pm ....

9am .... 4pm ....

10am .... 5pm ....

11am .... 6pm ....

12pm .... 7pm ....

....

....

....

....

....

....

....

....

....

....

....

....

....

Take three long deep breaths and smile.

Date: /   /   Time I woke up:

How would you rate your mood this morning? 0 1 2 3 4 5 6 7 8 9 10

Choose three power affirmations to raise your vibration:

♔ ....

♔ ....

♔ ....

Your Inner Queen always has a message for you.
Which words of encouragement does she need you to hear today?

♔ ....

....

The world is a beautiful place. List three reasons to be grateful today:

♔ ....

♔ ....

♔ ....

Choose three inspired actions to make today amazing:

♔ ....

♔ ....

♔ ....

If something tries to trip you up today, how will your Inner Queen handle it?

♔ ....

....

How will you celebrate yourself today?

♔ ....

Evening Reflection

How would you rate your mood this evening? 0 1 2 3 4 5 6 7 8 9 10

Today's big win: ....

Today's big lesson: ....

*'It takes strength to look at someone else's success and clap
for them without letting comparison creep in.'*

—*Megan Rose Lane*—

Daily Queen Habits

☐ MOVEMENT   ☐ STILLNESS   ☐ KINDNESS

6am ....   1pm ....

7am ....   2pm ....

8am ....   3pm ....

9am ....   4pm ....

10am ....   5pm ....

11am ....   6pm ....

12pm ....   7pm ....

....

....

....

....

....

....

....

....

....

....

....

....

Take three long deep breaths and smile.

Date: /   /   Time I woke up:

How would you rate your mood this morning? 0 1 2 3 4 5 6 7 8 9 10

Choose three power affirmations to raise your vibration:

♛ ....

♛ ....

♛ ....

Your Inner Queen always has a message for you.
Which words of encouragement does she need you to hear today?

♛ ....

....

The world is a beautiful place. List three reasons to be grateful today:

♛ ....

♛ ....

♛ ....

Choose three inspired actions to make today amazing:

♛ ....

♛ ....

♛ ....

If something tries to trip you up today, how will your Inner Queen handle it?

♛ ....

....

How will you celebrate yourself today?

♛ ....

Evening Reflection

How would you rate your mood this evening? 0 1 2 3 4 5 6 7 8 9 10

Today's big win: ....

Today's big lesson: ....

'When I am tired, I rest. I can't be a superwoman everyday.'

—Jada Pinkett Smith—

Daily Queen Habits

☐ MOVEMENT   ☐ STILLNESS   ☐ KINDNESS

6am ....   1pm ....

7am ....   2pm ....

8am ....   3pm ....

9am ....   4pm ....

10am ....   5pm ....

11am ....   6pm ....

12pm ....   7pm ....

....

....

....

....

....

....

....

....

....

....

....

....

....

30 Day Reflections

Looking back over the last month, what has changed for you?

....

....

....

....

....

My Biggest Win ....

....

My Biggest Lesson ....

....

Rate your overall commitment to this journal .... %

Which habit/s have you found easiest to build?

....

Which habit/s have you had most resistance to?

....

What are your goals for the next 30 days?

1. ....

2. ....

3. ....

141

Life Assessment

Rate where you feel you are in each area right now
(1 being low vibration and 10 being high vibe!)

Energy 1 2 3 4 5 6 7 8 9 10

I feel energised, healthy and I'm moving my body regularly.

Mental Health 1 2 3 4 5 6 7 8 9 10

I am compassionate towards myself and have a kind, uplifting inner dialogue.

Relationships/Love 1 2 3 4 5 6 7 8 9 10

I have a deep, meaningful and healthy connection with my partner. My relationship brings me joy and fulfilment. (If single: I have a deep, meaningful and healthy connection with myself. I nurture myself and show myself love.)

Purpose 1 2 3 4 5 6 7 8 9 10

I am finding my purpose in this world. I am committed to feeling fulfilled and excited by my life. I follow my heart and listen to my inner guidance.

Circle 1 2 3 4 5 6 7 8 9 10

I am surrounded by uplifting, supportive people who raise me higher and inspire me to be the best version of myself.

Self Care 1 2 3 4 5 6 7 8 9 10

I spend time taking care of myself, allowing myself to rest and recover and treat myself with loving kindness.

Connection 1 2 3 4 5 6 7 8 9 10

I feel a deep sense of connection to my Inner Queen. I understand that I am always being supported by the Universe and can ask for help and guidance whenever I need it.

Abundance 1 2 3 4 5 6 7 8 9 10

I see abundance all around me and understand that the Universe is overflowing with everything I could ever need to thrive. I am generous because I know that there is always enough to go around. I am open to receiving all of the goodness life has to offer.

Growth 1 2 3 4 5 6 7 8 9 10

I have the courage to try new things and pursue my dreams everyday. I use adversity to learn, grow and adapt, and I understand that growth is an integral part of my journey.

Your Inner Queen is rocking this.
Keep cheering her on!

Take three long deep breaths and smile.

Date: /   /   Time I woke up:

How would you rate your mood this morning? 0 1 2 3 4 5 6 7 8 9 10

Choose three power affirmations to raise your vibration:

♛ ....

♛ ....

♛ ....

Your Inner Queen always has a message for you.
Which words of encouragement does she need you to hear today?

♛ ....

....

The world is a beautiful place. List three reasons to be grateful today:

♛ ....

♛ ....

♛ ....

Choose three inspired actions to make today amazing:

♛ ....

♛ ....

♛ ....

If something tries to trip you up today, how will your Inner Queen handle it?

♛ ....

....

How will you celebrate yourself today?

♛ ....

Evening Reflection

How would you rate your mood this evening? 0 1 2 3 4 5 6 7 8 9 10

Today's big win: ....

Today's big lesson: ....

'Don't live life in the past lane.'

—Samantha Ettus—

Daily Queen Habits

☐ MOVEMENT   ☐ STILLNESS   ☐ KINDNESS

6am	1pm ....
7am	2pm ....
8am	3pm ....
9am	4pm ....
10am	5pm ....
11am	6pm ....
12pm	7pm ....

....

....

....

....

....

....

....

....

....

....

....

....

....

Take three long deep breaths and smile.

Date: /   /   Time I woke up:

How would you rate your mood this morning? 0 1 2 3 4 5 6 7 8 9 10

Choose three power affirmations to raise your vibration:

♔ ....

♔ ....

♔ ....

Your Inner Queen always has a message for you.
Which words of encouragement does she need you to hear today?

♔ ....

....

The world is a beautiful place. List three reasons to be grateful today:

♔ ....

♔ ....

♔ ....

Choose three inspired actions to make today amazing:

♔ ....

♔ ....

♔ ....

If something tries to trip you up today, how will your Inner Queen handle it?

♔ ....

....

How will you celebrate yourself today?

♔ ....

Evening Reflection

How would you rate your mood this evening? 0 1 2 3 4 5 6 7 8 9 10

Today's big win: ....

Today's big lesson: ....

'Our deepest fear is not that we are inadequate. Our deepest fear is that we are powerful beyond measure. It is our light, not our darkness that frightens us'

— Marianne Williamson—

Daily Queen Habits

☐ MOVEMENT   ☐ STILLNESS   ☐ KINDNESS

6am ....   1pm ....

7am ....   2pm ....

8am ....   3pm ....

9am ....   4pm ....

10am ....   5pm ....

11am ....   6pm ....

12pm ....   7pm ....

....

....

....

....

....

....

....

....

....

....

....

....

Take three long deep breaths and smile.

Date: /   /   Time I woke up:

How would you rate your mood this morning? 0 1 2 3 4 5 6 7 8 9 10

Choose three power affirmations to raise your vibration:

👑 ....

👑 ....

👑 ....

Your Inner Queen always has a message for you.
Which words of encouragement does she need you to hear today?

👑 ....

....

The world is a beautiful place. List three reasons to be grateful today:

👑 ....

👑 ....

👑 ....

Choose three inspired actions to make today amazing:

👑 ....

👑 ....

👑 ....

If something tries to trip you up today, how will your Inner Queen handle it?

👑 ....

....

How will you celebrate yourself today?

👑 ....

Evening Reflection

How would you rate your mood this evening? 0 1 2 3 4 5 6 7 8 9 10

Today's big win: ....

Today's big lesson: ....

'Abundance is not something we acquire, it is something we tune into.'

—*Wayne Dyer*—

Daily Queen Habits

☐ MOVEMENT   ☐ STILLNESS   ☐ KINDNESS

6am .... 1pm ....

7am .... 2pm ....

8am .... 3pm ....

9am .... 4pm ....

10am .... 5pm ....

11am .... 6pm ....

12pm .... 7pm ....

....

....

....

....

....

....

....

....

....

....

....

....

....

Take three long deep breaths and smile.

Date: /   /   Time I woke up:

How would you rate your mood this morning? 0 1 2 3 4 5 6 7 8 9 10

Choose three power affirmations to raise your vibration:

♛ ....

♛ ....

♛ ....

Your Inner Queen always has a message for you.
Which words of encouragement does she need you to hear today?

♛ ....

....

The world is a beautiful place. List three reasons to be grateful today:

♛ ....

♛ ....

♛ ....

Choose three inspired actions to make today amazing:

♛ ....

♛ ....

♛ ....

If something tries to trip you up today, how will your Inner Queen handle it?

♛ ....

....

How will you celebrate yourself today?

♛ ....

Evening Reflection

How would you rate your mood this evening? 0 1 2 3 4 5 6 7 8 9 10

Today's big win: ....

Today's big lesson: ....

'The only person you are destined to become is the person you decide to be.'

—Ralph Waldo Emerson—

Daily Queen Habits

☐ MOVEMENT   ☐ STILLNESS   ☐ KINDNESS

6am ....   1pm ....

7am ....   2pm ....

8am ....   3pm ....

9am ....   4pm ....

10am ....   5pm ....

11am ....   6pm ....

12pm ....   7pm ....

....

....

....

....

....

....

....

....

....

....

....

....

....

Take three long deep breaths and smile.

Date: /   /   Time I woke up:

How would you rate your mood this morning? 0 1 2 3 4 5 6 7 8 9 10

Choose three power affirmations to raise your vibration:

♛ ....

♛ ....

♛ ....

Your Inner Queen always has a message for you.
Which words of encouragement does she need you to hear today?

♛ ....

....

The world is a beautiful place. List three reasons to be grateful today:

♛ ....

♛ ....

♛ ....

Choose three inspired actions to make today amazing:

♛ ....

♛ ....

♛ ....

If something tries to trip you up today, how will your Inner Queen handle it?

♛ ....

....

How will you celebrate yourself today?

♛ ....

Evening Reflection

How would you rate your mood this evening? 0 1 2 3 4 5 6 7 8 9 10

Today's big win: ....

Today's big lesson: ....

'So often we pretend we have made a decision, when what we have actually done is sign up to try until it gets too uncomfortable.'

—Jen Sincero—

Daily Queen Habits

☐ MOVEMENT   ☐ STILLNESS   ☐ KINDNESS

6am	1pm ....
7am	2pm ....
8am	3pm ....
9am	4pm ....
10am	5pm ....
11am	6pm ....
12pm	7pm ....

....

....

....

....

....

....

....

....

....

....

....

....

Take three long deep breaths and smile.

Date: /   /   Time I woke up:

How would you rate your mood this morning? 0 1 2 3 4 5 6 7 8 9 10

Choose three power affirmations to raise your vibration:

♛ ....

♛ ....

♛ ....

Your Inner Queen always has a message for you.
Which words of encouragement does she need you to hear today?

♛ ....

....

The world is a beautiful place. List three reasons to be grateful today:

♛ ....

♛ ....

♛ ....

Choose three inspired actions to make today amazing:

♛ ....

♛ ....

♛ ....

If something tries to trip you up today, how will your Inner Queen handle it?

♛ ....

....

How will you celebrate yourself today?

♛ ....

Evening Reflection

How would you rate your mood this evening? 0 1 2 3 4 5 6 7 8 9 10

Today's big win: ....

Today's big lesson: ....

'The challenge is not to be perfect but to be whole.'

—Jane Fonda—

Daily Queen Habits

☐ MOVEMENT   ☐ STILLNESS   ☐ KINDNESS

6am ....   1pm ....

7am ....   2pm ....

8am ....   3pm ....

9am ....   4pm ....

10am ....   5pm ....

11am ....   6pm ....

12pm ....   7pm ....

....

....

....

....

....

....

....

....

....

....

....

....

....

Take three long deep breaths and smile.

Date: /   /   Time I woke up:

How would you rate your mood this morning? 0 1 2 3 4 5 6 7 8 9 10

Choose three power affirmations to raise your vibration:

♛ ....

♛ ....

♛ ....

Your Inner Queen always has a message for you.
Which words of encouragement does she need you to hear today?

♛ ....

....

The world is a beautiful place. List three reasons to be grateful today:

♛ ....

♛ ....

♛ ....

Choose three inspired actions to make today amazing:

♛ ....

♛ ....

♛ ....

If something tries to trip you up today, how will your Inner Queen handle it?

♛ ....

....

How will you celebrate yourself today?

♛ ....

Evening Reflection

How would you rate your mood this evening? 0 1 2 3 4 5 6 7 8 9 10

Today's big win: ....

Today's big lesson: ....

'If you don't get out of the box you were raised in,
you won't understand how much bigger the world is.'

—Angelia Jolie—

Daily Queen Habits

☐ MOVEMENT   ☐ STILLNESS   ☐ KINDNESS

6am .... 1pm ....

7am .... 2pm ....

8am .... 3pm ....

9am .... 4pm ....

10am .... 5pm ....

11am .... 6pm ....

12pm .... 7pm ....

....

....

....

....

....

....

....

....

....

....

....

....

Take three long deep breaths and smile.

Date: /   /   Time I woke up:

How would you rate your mood this morning? 0 1 2 3 4 5 6 7 8 9 10

Choose three power affirmations to raise your vibration:

♛ ....

♛ ....

♛ ....

Your Inner Queen always has a message for you.
Which words of encouragement does she need you to hear today?

♛ ....

....

The world is a beautiful place. List three reasons to be grateful today:

♛ ....

♛ ....

♛ ....

Choose three inspired actions to make today amazing:

♛ ....

♛ ....

♛ ....

If something tries to trip you up today, how will your Inner Queen handle it?

♛ ....

....

How will you celebrate yourself today?

♛ ....

Evening Reflection

How would you rate your mood this evening? 0 1 2 3 4 5 6 7 8 9 10

Today's big win: ....

Today's big lesson: ....

'If is one of the greatest gifts you can give yourself, to forgive. Forgive everybody.'

—Maya Angelou—

Daily Queen Habits

☐ MOVEMENT   ☐ STILLNESS   ☐ KINDNESS

6am	1pm ....
7am	2pm ....
8am	3pm ....
9am	4pm ....
10am	5pm ....
11am	6pm ....
12pm	7pm ....

....

....

....

....

....

....

....

....

....

....

....

....

....

....

Take three long deep breaths and smile.

Date: /   /   Time I woke up:

How would you rate your mood this morning? 0 1 2 3 4 5 6 7 8 9 10

Choose three power affirmations to raise your vibration:

👑 ....

👑 ....

👑 ....

Your Inner Queen always has a message for you.
Which words of encouragement does she need you to hear today?

👑 ....

....

The world is a beautiful place. List three reasons to be grateful today:

👑 ....

👑 ....

👑 ....

Choose three inspired actions to make today amazing:

👑 ....

👑 ....

👑 ....

If something tries to trip you up today, how will your Inner Queen handle it?

👑 ....

....

How will you celebrate yourself today?

👑 ....

Evening Reflection

How would you rate your mood this evening? 0 1 2 3 4 5 6 7 8 9 10

Today's big win: ....

Today's big lesson: ....

'You can be the lead in your own life.'

—*Kerry Washington*—

Daily Queen Habits

☐ MOVEMENT   ☐ STILLNESS   ☐ KINDNESS

6am ....   1pm ....

7am ....   2pm ....

8am ....   3pm ....

9am ....   4pm ....

10am ....   5pm ....

11am ....   6pm ....

12pm ....   7pm ....

....

....

....

....

....

....

....

....

....

....

....

....

....

Take three long deep breaths and smile.

Date: /   /   Time I woke up:

How would you rate your mood this morning? 0 1 2 3 4 5 6 7 8 9 10

Choose three power affirmations to raise your vibration:

👑 ....

👑 ....

👑 ....

Your Inner Queen always has a message for you.
Which words of encouragement does she need you to hear today?

👑 ....

....

The world is a beautiful place. List three reasons to be grateful today:

👑 ....

👑 ....

👑 ....

Choose three inspired actions to make today amazing:

👑 ....

👑 ....

👑 ....

If something tries to trip you up today, how will your Inner Queen handle it?

👑 ....

....

How will you celebrate yourself today?

👑 ....

Evening Reflection

How would you rate your mood this evening? 0 1 2 3 4 5 6 7 8 9 10

Today's big win: ....

Today's big lesson: ....

'We do not need magic to change the world, we carry all the power we need inside ourselves already; we have the power to imagine better.'

—J.K. Rowling—

Daily Queen Habits

☐ MOVEMENT   ☐ STILLNESS   ☐ KINDNESS

6am .... 1pm ....

7am .... 2pm ....

8am .... 3pm ....

9am .... 4pm ....

10am .... 5pm ....

11am .... 6pm ....

12pm .... 7pm ....

....

....

....

....

....

....

....

....

....

....

....

....

Take three long deep breaths and smile.

Date: /   /   Time I woke up:

How would you rate your mood this morning? 0 1 2 3 4 5 6 7 8 9 10

Choose three power affirmations to raise your vibration:

👑 ....

👑 ....

👑 ....

Your Inner Queen always has a message for you.
Which words of encouragement does she need you to hear today?

👑 ....

....

The world is a beautiful place. List three reasons to be grateful today:

👑 ....

👑 ....

👑 ....

Choose three inspired actions to make today amazing:

👑 ....

👑 ....

👑 ....

If something tries to trip you up today, how will your Inner Queen handle it?

👑 ....

....

How will you celebrate yourself today?

👑 ....

Evening Reflection

How would you rate your mood this evening? 0 1 2 3 4 5 6 7 8 9 10

Today's big win: ....

Today's big lesson: ....

'Get brave, really brave and start doing the work for you.'
—The Completion Coach—

Daily Queen Habits

☐ MOVEMENT   ☐ STILLNESS   ☐ KINDNESS

6am	....	1pm	....
7am	....	2pm	....
8am	....	3pm	....
9am	....	4pm	....
10am	....	5pm	....
11am	....	6pm	....
12pm	....	7pm	....

Take three long deep breaths and smile.

Date: /   /   Time I woke up:

How would you rate your mood this morning? 0 1 2 3 4 5 6 7 8 9 10

Choose three power affirmations to raise your vibration:

♛ ....

♛ ....

♛ ....

Your Inner Queen always has a message for you.
Which words of encouragement does she need you to hear today?

♛ ....

....

The world is a beautiful place. List three reasons to be grateful today:

♛ ....

♛ ....

♛ ....

Choose three inspired actions to make today amazing:

♛ ....

♛ ....

♛ ....

If something tries to trip you up today, how will your Inner Queen handle it?

♛ ....

....

How will you celebrate yourself today?

♛ ....

Evening Reflection

How would you rate your mood this evening? 0 1 2 3 4 5 6 7 8 9 10

Today's big win: ....

Today's big lesson: ....

'Clap louder for everyone else, because we all deserve to be celebrated and another humans happiness should never take away from our own.'

—Megan Rose Lane—

Daily Queen Habits

☐ MOVEMENT   ☐ STILLNESS   ☐ KINDNESS

6am .... 1pm ....

7am .... 2pm ....

8am .... 3pm ....

9am .... 4pm ....

10am .... 5pm ....

11am .... 6pm ....

12pm .... 7pm ....

....

....

....

....

....

....

....

....

....

....

....

....

Take three long deep breaths and smile.

Date: /   /   Time I woke up:

How would you rate your mood this morning? 0 1 2 3 4 5 6 7 8 9 10

Choose three power affirmations to raise your vibration:

👑 ....

👑 ....

👑 ....

Your Inner Queen always has a message for you.
Which words of encouragement does she need you to hear today?

👑 ....

....

The world is a beautiful place. List three reasons to be grateful today:

👑 ....

👑 ....

👑 ....

Choose three inspired actions to make today amazing:

👑 ....

👑 ....

👑 ....

If something tries to trip you up today, how will your Inner Queen handle it?

👑 ....

....

How will you celebrate yourself today?

👑 ....

Evening Reflection

How would you rate your mood this evening? 0 1 2 3 4 5 6 7 8 9 10

Today's big win: ....

Today's big lesson: ....

'And the day came when the risk to remain tight in a bud
was more painful than the risk it took to blossom.'

—*Anais Nin*—

Daily Queen Habits

☐ MOVEMENT   ☐ STILLNESS   ☐ KINDNESS

6am .... 1pm ....

7am .... 2pm ....

8am .... 3pm ....

9am .... 4pm ....

10am .... 5pm ....

11am .... 6pm ....

12pm .... 7pm ....

....

....

....

....

....

....

....

....

....

....

....

....

Take three long deep breaths and smile.

Date: /   /   Time I woke up:

How would you rate your mood this morning? 0 1 2 3 4 5 6 7 8 9 10

Choose three power affirmations to raise your vibration:

♔ ....

♔ ....

♔ ....

Your Inner Queen always has a message for you.
Which words of encouragement does she need you to hear today?

♔ ....

....

The world is a beautiful place. List three reasons to be grateful today:

♔ ....

♔ ....

♔ ....

Choose three inspired actions to make today amazing:

♔ ....

♔ ....

♔ ....

If something tries to trip you up today, how will your Inner Queen handle it?

♔ ....

....

How will you celebrate yourself today?

♔ ....

Evening Reflection

How would you rate your mood this evening? 0 1 2 3 4 5 6 7 8 9 10

Today's big win: ....

Today's big lesson: ....

'Conflict cannot survive without your participation.'

Daily Queen Habits

☐ MOVEMENT   ☐ STILLNESS   ☐ KINDNESS

6am ....   1pm ....

7am ....   2pm ....

8am ....   3pm ....

9am ....   4pm ....

10am ....   5pm ....

11am ....   6pm ....

12pm ....   7pm ....

....

....

....

....

....

....

....

....

....

....

....

....

....

....

Take three long deep breaths and smile.

Date: /   /   Time I woke up:

How would you rate your mood this morning? 0 1 2 3 4 5 6 7 8 9 10

Choose three power affirmations to raise your vibration:

👑 ....

👑 ....

👑 ....

Your Inner Queen always has a message for you.
Which words of encouragement does she need you to hear today?

👑 ....

....

The world is a beautiful place. List three reasons to be grateful today:

👑 ....

👑 ....

👑 ....

Choose three inspired actions to make today amazing:

👑 ....

👑 ....

👑 ....

If something tries to trip you up today, how will your Inner Queen handle it?

👑 ....

....

How will you celebrate yourself today?

👑 ....

Evening Reflection

How would you rate your mood this evening? 0 1 2 3 4 5 6 7 8 9 10

Today's big win: ....

Today's big lesson: ....

'A memory without the emotional charge is called wisdom.'

—*Joe Dispenza*—

Daily Queen Habits

☐ MOVEMENT   ☐ STILLNESS   ☐ KINDNESS

6am .... 1pm ....

7am .... 2pm ....

8am .... 3pm ....

9am .... 4pm ....

10am .... 5pm ....

11am .... 6pm ....

12pm .... 7pm ....

....

....

....

....

....

....

....

....

....

....

....

....

....

Take three long deep breaths and smile.

Date: /   /   Time I woke up:

How would you rate your mood this morning? 0 1 2 3 4 5 6 7 8 9 10

Choose three power affirmations to raise your vibration:

♔ ....

♔ ....

♔ ....

Your Inner Queen always has a message for you.
Which words of encouragement does she need you to hear today?

♔ ....

....

The world is a beautiful place. List three reasons to be grateful today:

♔ ....

♔ ....

♔ ....

Choose three inspired actions to make today amazing:

♔ ....

♔ ....

♔ ....

If something tries to trip you up today, how will your Inner Queen handle it?

♔ ....

....

How will you celebrate yourself today?

♔ ....

Evening Reflection

How would you rate your mood this evening? 0 1 2 3 4 5 6 7 8 9 10

Today's big win: ....

Today's big lesson: ....

'Cause I'm my own soulmate.'

—Lizzo—

Daily Queen Habits

☐ MOVEMENT   ☐ STILLNESS   ☐ KINDNESS

6am ....   1pm ....

7am ....   2pm ....

8am ....   3pm ....

9am ....   4pm ....

10am ....   5pm ....

11am ....   6pm ....

12pm ....   7pm ....

....

....

....

....

....

....

....

....

....

....

....

....

Take three long deep breaths and smile.

Date: / /   Time I woke up:

How would you rate your mood this morning? 0 1 2 3 4 5 6 7 8 9 10

Choose three power affirmations to raise your vibration:

♔ ....

♔ ....

♔ ....

Your Inner Queen always has a message for you.
Which words of encouragement does she need you to hear today?

♔ ....

....

The world is a beautiful place. List three reasons to be grateful today:

♔ ....

♔ ....

♔ ....

Choose three inspired actions to make today amazing:

♔ ....

♔ ....

♔ ....

If something tries to trip you up today, how will your Inner Queen handle it?

♔ ....

....

How will you celebrate yourself today?

♔ ....

Evening Reflection

How would you rate your mood this evening? 0 1 2 3 4 5 6 7 8 9 10

Today's big win: ....

Today's big lesson: ....

*'You either walk inside your story and own it or you stand
outside your story and hustle for your worthiness.'*

—Brene Brown—

Daily Queen Habits

☐ MOVEMENT ☐ STILLNESS ☐ KINDNESS

6am .... 1pm ....

7am .... 2pm ....

8am .... 3pm ....

9am .... 4pm ....

10am .... 5pm ....

11am .... 6pm ....

12pm .... 7pm ....

....

....

....

....

....

....

....

....

....

....

....

....

Take three long deep breaths and smile.

Date: /   /   Time I woke up:

How would you rate your mood this morning? 0 1 2 3 4 5 6 7 8 9 10

Choose three power affirmations to raise your vibration:

♛ ....

♛ ....

♛ ....

Your Inner Queen always has a message for you.
Which words of encouragement does she need you to hear today?

♛ ....

....

The world is a beautiful place. List three reasons to be grateful today:

♛ ....

♛ ....

♛ ....

Choose three inspired actions to make today amazing:

♛ ....

♛ ....

♛ ....

If something tries to trip you up today, how will your Inner Queen handle it?

♛ ....

....

How will you celebrate yourself today?

♛ ....

Evening Reflection

How would you rate your mood this evening? 0 1 2 3 4 5 6 7 8 9 10

Today's big win: ....

Today's big lesson: ....

179

*'I expand in abundance, success, and love every day,
as I inspire those around me to do the same.'*

—*Gay Hendricks*—

Daily Queen Habits

☐ MOVEMENT   ☐ STILLNESS   ☐ KINDNESS

6am .... 1pm ....

7am .... 2pm ....

8am .... 3pm ....

9am .... 4pm ....

10am .... 5pm ....

11am .... 6pm ....

12pm .... 7pm ....

....

....

....

....

....

....

....

....

....

....

....

....

Take three long deep breaths and smile.

Date: /   /   Time I woke up:

How would you rate your mood this morning? 0 1 2 3 4 5 6 7 8 9 10

Choose three power affirmations to raise your vibration:

♛ ....

♛ ....

♛ ....

Your Inner Queen always has a message for you.
Which words of encouragement does she need you to hear today?

♛ ....

....

The world is a beautiful place. List three reasons to be grateful today:

♛ ....

♛ ....

♛ ....

Choose three inspired actions to make today amazing:

♛ ....

♛ ....

♛ ....

If something tries to trip you up today, how will your Inner Queen handle it?

♛ ....

....

How will you celebrate yourself today?

♛ ....

Evening Reflection

How would you rate your mood this evening? 0 1 2 3 4 5 6 7 8 9 10

Today's big win: ....

Today's big lesson: ....

'Never forget that once upon a time, in an unguarded moment,
you recognized yourself as a friend'

—Elizabeth Gilbert—

Daily Queen Habits

☐ MOVEMENT   ☐ STILLNESS   ☐ KINDNESS

6am ....   1pm ....

7am ....   2pm ....

8am ....   3pm ....

9am ....   4pm ....

10am ....   5pm ....

11am ....   6pm ....

12pm ....   7pm ....

....

....

....

....

....

....

....

....

....

....

....

....

Take three long deep breaths and smile.

Date: /   /   Time I woke up:

How would you rate your mood this morning? 0 1 2 3 4 5 6 7 8 9 10

Choose three power affirmations to raise your vibration:

♛ ....

♛ ....

♛ ....

Your Inner Queen always has a message for you.
Which words of encouragement does she need you to hear today?

♛ ....

....

The world is a beautiful place. List three reasons to be grateful today:

♛ ....

♛ ....

♛ ....

Choose three inspired actions to make today amazing:

♛ ....

♛ ....

♛ ....

If something tries to trip you up today, how will your Inner Queen handle it?

♛ ....

....

How will you celebrate yourself today?

♛ ....

Evening Reflection

How would you rate your mood this evening? 0 1 2 3 4 5 6 7 8 9 10

Today's big win: ....

Today's big lesson: ....

*'When we forget to make sure we are doing okay,
we can't then give our best to the people we care about.'*

—*Fearne Cotton*—

Daily Queen Habits

☐ MOVEMENT   ☐ STILLNESS   ☐ KINDNESS

6am ....

7am ....

8am ....

9am ....

10am ....

11am ....

12pm ....

1pm ....

2pm ....

3pm ....

4pm ....

5pm ....

6pm ....

7pm ....

....

....

....

....

....

....

....

....

....

....

....

....

Take three long deep breaths and smile.

Date: /   /   Time I woke up:

How would you rate your mood this morning? 0 1 2 3 4 5 6 7 8 9 10

Choose three power affirmations to raise your vibration:

♛ ....

♛ ....

♛ ....

Your Inner Queen always has a message for you.
Which words of encouragement does she need you to hear today?

♛ ....

....

The world is a beautiful place. List three reasons to be grateful today:

♛ ....

♛ ....

♛ ....

Choose three inspired actions to make today amazing:

♛ ....

♛ ....

♛ ....

If something tries to trip you up today, how will your Inner Queen handle it?

♛ ....

....

How will you celebrate yourself today?

♛ ....

Evening Reflection

How would you rate your mood this evening? 0 1 2 3 4 5 6 7 8 9 10

Today's big win: ....

Today's big lesson: ....

'The most powerful words in the universe are the words you say to yourself.'

—Marie Forleo—

Daily Queen Habits

☐ MOVEMENT   ☐ STILLNESS   ☐ KINDNESS

6am ....

7am ....

8am ....

9am ....

10am ....

11am ....

12pm ....

1pm ....

2pm ....

3pm ....

4pm ....

5pm ....

6pm ....

7pm ....

....

....

....

....

....

....

....

....

....

....

....

....

....

Take three long deep breaths and smile.

Date: /   /   Time I woke up:

How would you rate your mood this morning? 0 1 2 3 4 5 6 7 8 9 10

Choose three power affirmations to raise your vibration:

👑 ....

👑 ....

👑 ....

Your Inner Queen always has a message for you.
Which words of encouragement does she need you to hear today?

👑 ....

....

The world is a beautiful place. List three reasons to be grateful today:

👑 ....

👑 ....

👑 ....

Choose three inspired actions to make today amazing:

👑 ....

👑 ....

👑 ....

If something tries to trip you up today, how will your Inner Queen handle it?

👑 ....

....

How will you celebrate yourself today?

👑 ....

Evening Reflection

How would you rate your mood this evening? 0 1 2 3 4 5 6 7 8 9 10

Today's big win: ....

Today's big lesson: ....

Isn't it marvelous to discover that you're the one you've been waiting for? That you are your own freedom?"

—Byron Katie—

Daily Queen Habits

☐ MOVEMENT   ☐ STILLNESS   ☐ KINDNESS

6am ....   1pm ....

7am ....   2pm ....

8am ....   3pm ....

9am ....   4pm ....

10am ....   5pm ....

11am ....   6pm ....

12pm ....   7pm ....

....

....

....

....

....

....

....

....

....

....

....

....

Take three long deep breaths and smile.

Date: /   /   Time I woke up:

How would you rate your mood this morning? 0 1 2 3 4 5 6 7 8 9 10

Choose three power affirmations to raise your vibration:

👑 ....

👑 ....

👑 ....

Your Inner Queen always has a message for you.
Which words of encouragement does she need you to hear today?

👑 ....

....

The world is a beautiful place. List three reasons to be grateful today:

👑 ....

👑 ....

👑 ....

Choose three inspired actions to make today amazing:

👑 ....

👑 ....

👑 ....

If something tries to trip you up today, how will your Inner Queen handle it?

👑 ....

....

How will you celebrate yourself today?

👑 ....

Evening Reflection

How would you rate your mood this evening? 0 1 2 3 4 5 6 7 8 9 10

Today's big win: ....

Today's big lesson: ....

'Usually when I feel like there's no time, it really means I haven't made time for myself.'

—*Gay Hendricks*—

Daily Queen Habits

☐ MOVEMENT   ☐ STILLNESS   ☐ KINDNESS

6am .... 1pm ....

7am .... 2pm ....

8am .... 3pm ....

9am .... 4pm ....

10am .... 5pm ....

11am .... 6pm ....

12pm .... 7pm ....

....

....

....

....

....

....

....

....

....

....

....

....

....

Take three long deep breaths and smile.

Date: /   /   Time I woke up:

How would you rate your mood this morning? 0 1 2 3 4 5 6 7 8 9 10

Choose three power affirmations to raise your vibration:

👑 ....

👑 ....

👑 ....

Your Inner Queen always has a message for you.
Which words of encouragement does she need you to hear today?

👑 ....

....

The world is a beautiful place. List three reasons to be grateful today:

👑 ....

👑 ....

👑 ....

Choose three inspired actions to make today amazing:

👑 ....

👑 ....

👑 ....

If something tries to trip you up today, how will your Inner Queen handle it?

👑 ....

....

How will you celebrate yourself today?

👑 ....

Evening Reflection

How would you rate your mood this evening? 0 1 2 3 4 5 6 7 8 9 10

Today's big win: ....

Today's big lesson: ....

'We don't realize that, somewhere within us all,
there does exist a supreme self who is eternally at peace.'

—Elizabeth Gilbert—

Daily Queen Habits

☐ MOVEMENT   ☐ STILLNESS   ☐ KINDNESS

6am .... 1pm ....

7am .... 2pm ....

8am .... 3pm ....

9am .... 4pm ....

10am .... 5pm ....

11am .... 6pm ....

12pm .... 7pm ....

....

....

....

....

....

....

....

....

....

....

....

....

Take three long deep breaths and smile.

Date: /   /   Time I woke up:

How would you rate your mood this morning? 0 1 2 3 4 5 6 7 8 9 10

Choose three power affirmations to raise your vibration:

♔ ....

♔ ....

♔ ....

Your Inner Queen always has a message for you.
Which words of encouragement does she need you to hear today?

♔ ....

....

The world is a beautiful place. List three reasons to be grateful today:

♔ ....

♔ ....

♔ ....

Choose three inspired actions to make today amazing:

♔ ....

♔ ....

♔ ....

If something tries to trip you up today, how will your Inner Queen handle it?

♔ ....

....

How will you celebrate yourself today?

♔ ....

Evening Reflection

How would you rate your mood this evening? 0 1 2 3 4 5 6 7 8 9 10

Today's big win: ....

Today's big lesson: ....

193

*'What's the greater risk? Letting go of what people think —
or letting go of how I feel, what I believe, and who I am?.'*

—Brene Brown—

Daily Queen Habits

☐ MOVEMENT   ☐ STILLNESS   ☐ KINDNESS

6am .... 1pm ....

7am .... 2pm ....

8am .... 3pm ....

9am .... 4pm ....

10am .... 5pm ....

11am .... 6pm ....

12pm .... 7pm ....

....

....

....

....

....

....

....

....

....

....

....

....

Take three long deep breaths and smile.

Date: /   /   Time I woke up:

How would you rate your mood this morning? 0 1 2 3 4 5 6 7 8 9 10

Choose three power affirmations to raise your vibration:

👑 ....

👑 ....

👑 ....

Your Inner Queen always has a message for you.
Which words of encouragement does she need you to hear today?

👑 ....

....

The world is a beautiful place. List three reasons to be grateful today:

👑 ....

👑 ....

👑 ....

Choose three inspired actions to make today amazing:

👑 ....

👑 ....

👑 ....

If something tries to trip you up today, how will your Inner Queen handle it?

👑 ....

....

How will you celebrate yourself today?

👑 ....

Evening Reflection

How would you rate your mood this evening? 0 1 2 3 4 5 6 7 8 9 10

Today's big win: ....

Today's big lesson: ....

'I win or I learn, but I never lose.'

—Marie Forleo—

Daily Queen Habits

☐ MOVEMENT   ☐ STILLNESS   ☐ KINDNESS

6am ....   1pm ....

7am ....   2pm ....

8am ....   3pm ....

9am ....   4pm ....

10am ....   5pm ....

11am ....   6pm ....

12pm ....   7pm ....

....

....

....

....

....

....

....

....

....

....

....

....

....

Take three long deep breaths and smile.

Date: /   /   Time I woke up:

How would you rate your mood this morning? 0 1 2 3 4 5 6 7 8 9 10

Choose three power affirmations to raise your vibration:

♛ ....

♛ ....

♛ ....

Your Inner Queen always has a message for you.
Which words of encouragement does she need you to hear today?

♛ ....

  ....

The world is a beautiful place. List three reasons to be grateful today:

♛ ....

♛ ....

♛ ....

Choose three inspired actions to make today amazing:

♛ ....

♛ ....

♛ ....

If something tries to trip you up today, how will your Inner Queen handle it?

♛ ....

  ....

How will you celebrate yourself today?

♛ ....

Evening Reflection

How would you rate your mood this evening? 0 1 2 3 4 5 6 7 8 9 10

Today's big win: ....

Today's big lesson: ....

'The journey starts with a single step—not with thinking about taking a step.'

—Jeff Olson—

Daily Queen Habits

☐ MOVEMENT   ☐ STILLNESS   ☐ KINDNESS

6am ....   1pm ....

7am ....   2pm ....

8am ....   3pm ....

9am ....   4pm ....

10am ....   5pm ....

11am ....   6pm ....

12pm ....   7pm ....

....

....

....

....

....

....

....

....

....

....

....

....

Take three long deep breaths and smile.

Date: /   /   Time I woke up:

How would you rate your mood this morning? 0 1 2 3 4 5 6 7 8 9 10

Choose three power affirmations to raise your vibration:

♛ ....

♛ ....

♛ ....

Your Inner Queen always has a message for you.
Which words of encouragement does she need you to hear today?

♛ ....

   ....

The world is a beautiful place. List three reasons to be grateful today:

♛ ....

♛ ....

♛ ....

Choose three inspired actions to make today amazing:

♛ ....

♛ ....

♛ ....

If something tries to trip you up today, how will your Inner Queen handle it?

♛ ....

   ....

How will you celebrate yourself today?

♛ ....

Evening Reflection

How would you rate your mood this evening? 0 1 2 3 4 5 6 7 8 9 10

Today's big win: ....

Today's big lesson: ....

'Doing what you've been doing is going to get you what you've been getting.'

—*Seth Godin*

Daily Queen Habits

☐ MOVEMENT   ☐ STILLNESS   ☐ KINDNESS

6am .... 1pm ....

7am .... 2pm ....

8am .... 3pm ....

9am .... 4pm ....

10am .... 5pm ....

11am .... 6pm ....

12pm .... 7pm ....

....

....

....

....

....

....

....

....

....

....

....

....

....

Take three long deep breaths and smile.

Date: /   /   Time I woke up:

How would you rate your mood this morning? 0 1 2 3 4 5 6 7 8 9 10

Choose three power affirmations to raise your vibration:

♛ ....

♛ ....

♛ ....

Your Inner Queen always has a message for you.
Which words of encouragement does she need you to hear today?

♛ ....

....

The world is a beautiful place. List three reasons to be grateful today:

♛ ....

♛ ....

♛ ....

Choose three inspired actions to make today amazing:

♛ ....

♛ ....

♛ ....

If something tries to trip you up today, how will your Inner Queen handle it?

♛ ....

....

How will you celebrate yourself today?

♛ ....

Evening Reflection

How would you rate your mood this evening? 0 1 2 3 4 5 6 7 8 9 10

Today's big win: ....

Today's big lesson: ....

'Your past does not equal your future.'

Daily Queen Habits

☐ MOVEMENT   ☐ STILLNESS   ☐ KINDNESS

6am ....   1pm ....

7am ....   2pm ....

8am ....   3pm ....

9am ....   4pm ....

10am ....   5pm ....

11am ....   6pm ....

12pm ....   7pm ....

....

....

....

....

....

....

....

....

....

....

....

....

....

....

....

Take three long deep breaths and smile.

Date: /   /   Time I woke up:

How would you rate your mood this morning? 0 1 2 3 4 5 6 7 8 9 10

Choose three power affirmations to raise your vibration:

♛ ....

♛ ....

♛ ....

Your Inner Queen always has a message for you.
Which words of encouragement does she need you to hear today?

♛ ....

....

The world is a beautiful place. List three reasons to be grateful today:

♛ ....

♛ ....

♛ ....

Choose three inspired actions to make today amazing:

♛ ....

♛ ....

♛ ....

If something tries to trip you up today, how will your Inner Queen handle it?

♛ ....

....

How will you celebrate yourself today?

♛ ....

Evening Reflection

How would you rate your mood this evening? 0 1 2 3 4 5 6 7 8 9 10

Today's big win: ....

Today's big lesson: ....

203

*'The only thing that's keeping you from getting what
you want is the story you keep telling yourself.'*

—*Tony Robbins*—

Daily Queen Habits

☐ MOVEMENT　　　　　☐ STILLNESS　　　　　☐ KINDNESS

6am .... 1pm ....

7am .... 2pm ....

8am .... 3pm ....

9am .... 4pm ....

10am .... 5pm ....

11am .... 6pm ....

12pm .... 7pm ....

....

....

....

....

....

....

....

....

....

....

....

....

30 Day Reflections

Looking back over the last month, what has changed for you?

....
....
....
....
....
....

My Biggest Win ....
....

My Biggest Lesson ....
....

Rate your overall commitment to this journal .... %

Which habit/s have you found easiest to build?
....

Which habit/s have you had most resistance to?
....

What are your goals for the next 30 days?
1. ....
2. ....
3. ....

Life Assessment

Rate where you feel you are in each area right now
(1 being low vibration and 10 being high vibe!)

Energy   1   2   3   4   5   6   7   8   9   10
I feel energised, healthy and I'm moving my body regularly.

Mental Health   1   2   3   4   5   6   7   8   9   10
I am compassionate towards myself and have a kind, uplifting inner dialogue.

Relationships/Love   1   2   3   4   5   6   7   8   9   10
I have a deep, meaningful and healthy connection with my partner. My relationship brings me joy and fulfilment. (If single: I have a deep, meaningful and healthy connection with myself. I nurture myself and show myself love.)

Purpose   1   2   3   4   5   6   7   8   9   10
I am finding my purpose in this world. I am committed to feeling fulfilled and excited by my life. I follow my heart and listen to my inner guidance.

Circle   1   2   3   4   5   6   7   8   9   10
I am surrounded by uplifting, supportive people who raise me higher and inspire me to be the best version of myself.

Self Care   1   2   3   4   5   6   7   8   9   10
I spend time taking care of myself, allowing myself to rest and recover and treat myself with loving kindness.

Connection   1   2   3   4   5   6   7   8   9   10
I feel a deep sense of connection to my Inner Queen. I understand that I am always being supported by the Universe and can ask for help and guidance whenever I need it.

Abundance   1   2   3   4   5   6   7   8   9   10
I see abundance all around me and understand that the Universe is overflowing with everything I could ever need to thrive. I am generous because I know that there is always enough to go around. I am open to receiving all of the goodness life has to offer.

Growth   1   2   3   4   5   6   7   8   9   10
I have the courage to try new things and pursue my dreams everyday. I use adversity to learn, grow and adapt, and I understand that growth is an integral part of my journey.

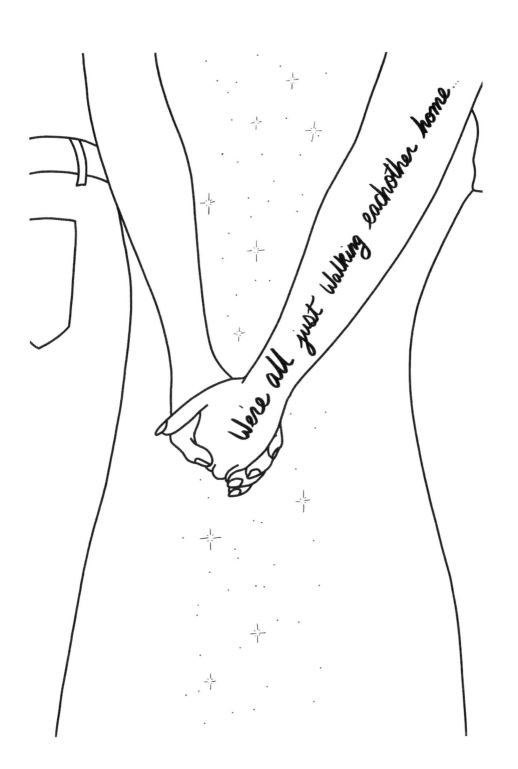

Wobbles

Acceptance

The inability to fully accept ourselves is a shared human experience. You're not alone in the struggle to feel completely at peace with who you are; from your appearance to your personality, your life circumstances, relationships, career and the cards you were dealt. Life can often feel quite unfair, especially when immersed in a culture that floods our minds with unrealistic images of airbrushed models, convincing us that we must 'be more like them' in order to be loved and accepted by society. The mass media portrays an impossible standard of existence, one that cannot be attained by even the most willing and devoted human being. You can spend all of your time, money and energy trying to be perfect – but please know that this is an endless and exhausting pursuit for something that simply is not possible. When we get stuck in comparison mode, our sense of self-worth can take a painful nose-dive into the land of resistance. You see, if you're not accepting something – you are choosing to resist it. You are arguing with reality, and frustration is an inevitable outcome. Many of us spend a great deal of time regretting our past mistakes, dwelling on the way we acted and wishing we could turn back the clock to do things differently. The key to acceptance really does lie in the art of letting go. Letting go of the past, of expectation, comparison and self-deprecating thoughts and beliefs. It's time to quieten the ego that's constantly telling us we must do, be and have more in order to feel happy and at peace within ourselves. We also tend to fear that if we accept ourselves, we will become stuck and never change or grow, but this simply isn't the case. Acceptance is the ultimate foundation for on which to grow and improve ourselves. If you can't accept yourself now, you won't accept yourself 'when' either.

Affirmation

I relax into acceptance of all that I am and know that it is enough. I am always enough.

Action

Rub your heart clockwise, close your eyes and repeat over and over again "I am enough, I am safe, I am loved". Take 3 long, deep breaths and really feel your heart beating. Relax your jaw, drop the tongue from the roof of your mouth and relax your shoulders. Continue to rub your heart and repeat your mantra.

Anxiety

Anxiety is one of the most debilitating emotions a human can experience and has a complicated network of reasons behind why it may show up in your life. While we can never generalise why you may be feeling a sense of unease, worry, or panic, what we can say is that when experiencing anxiety, your mind has drifted from the present moment and is mentally living in the future.

Since the future does not exist and is purely a figment of your imagination, you can rest assured that whatever scenario you've made up in your head...is exactly that. Made up. It's not real, it hasn't actually happened and there's no real evidence that it will. The tricky thing is, your brain cannot tell what's actually happening in real time and what is an imagined scenario in your mind, and so the worst-case-scenario you're picturing sends your body into 'fight or flight' mode. This is survival mode and has been cleverly designed for your protection so that you can run away from or fight off whatever danger lies before you. The stress hormones released during these moments are supposed to give you a surge of energy for you to use in order to survive. However, when there's no real danger in the present moment, there's no real use for this surge of adrenaline and you end up with side effects such as sweating, shaking and hyperventilating. This feeling in itself can be really frightening, and actually cause us to feel even more anxiety. Many people develop a fear of fear itself, and become anxious about being anxious – which can be an incredibly confusing emotion to process.

It's really important to understand that you are neither your thoughts, nor your emotions. "You are the sky, everything else is just the weather" is an incredible quote to live by. Your natural state of being is peaceful, and when you allow any thoughts and emotions to drift through your mind like passing clouds – everything becomes still and the anxiety melts away.

Another powerful way to cope with anxiety is through acceptance. Resistance to any emotion just creates further stress, so by leaning into the feeling, acknowledging its presence and allowing it to be felt actually causes it to disappear. Since anxiety is trying to protect you and keep you safe, you can choose to see it as a friend instead of an enemy. Say hello when it arrives, thank it for coming, and then remind the anxiety that you are safe – so it needn't hang around too long. Don't try to push it away, just allow it to be there whilst reminding yourself that you are entirely separate from it. Anxiety always passes, and it cannot hurt you. It's JUST a feeling.

Affirmations

I am not my anxiety. I just have anxious moments and they always pass.

I am the sky, everything else is just the weather.

I am safe.

Action

Practice a meditation. If you find your breathing is faster than normal, then breathe in for four, hold for two and out for six. Do this several times to slow down your breathing and really ground yourself back into your body.

Feeling Behind in Life

Society absolutely loves to make us feel like we are getting 'left behind' and simply never quite keeping up with everybody else. Feeling like we're late to the party is a common concern, and to be expected when we place so much importance on achieving particular life goals by a certain age. But the fictional "life stages" are an incredibly futile way to measure our own personal success and can lead us to making major life choices based on fear, instead of being lead by our powerful intuition. There is no rule book in this life, and we are all on our own paths, destined for vastly different yet infinitely wonderful things. Let's take for example the misconception that failing to be married before the age of 30 suddenly means you've failed at life. Huh?! We come up with the most ridiculous reasons to believe that we are worthless. These shallow and trivial 'rules' do not define us. They define society for its cruel and twisted way of making us compete with one another and constantly feel like we must 'keep up' or 'get ahead'. Life is not a competition. Understand that you are exactly where you need to be, right in this very moment. Whatever you are going through right now, whatever worries or self-defeating beliefs you continue to entertain in your life – just know that you do not need them. They serve you absolutely no purpose and do nothing but hold you back.

It's time to own your path. It's time to stop comparing where you're at with everybody else, and trust that your journey is wonderfully unique, and will unfold in perfect time if you just trust and allow it to be where it's at.

Affirmation

I trust the timing of life and recognise that I am truly on my own path, in my own time. I can never be late in my own life.

Action

Create a vision board that you really FEEL. Put words on it, pictures, things that really make you smile. Make it something that you look at daily and think "how do I show up for this". This can be down to the way you think that day, the words you use, the way you dress, how you show up in confidence, how you allocate the money you do have, how you speak to yourself or what time you get up/go to bed. Sit with the board and really feel what life is like through this vision, and then start showing up for it in total belief that you are capable of achieving it all.

Setting Boundaries

Boundaries are the invisible walls we build around our energy, which dictate the way in which we allow ourselves to be treated by other people. If you're the type of person who constantly says 'yes' when they really want to say 'no', if you have a hard time standing up for yourself and allow people to be bossy, pushy and rude to you, or if you're constantly running on empty from putting the needs of others before your own… it's most definitely time to create some stronger boundaries for yourself. You deserve to feel completely able to do what is right for you, even if it may disappoint someone else. By having clear boundaries in place, you take away the need to constantly please other people, and instead choose to value yourself more. It's important to pay close attention to the situations where you feel a knot in your stomach, you may feel anxious, tired, or want to cry. Identifying where you need more space, more self-respect, or the power to speak your mind and say 'no' is the first step.

Boundaries are not set in stone – you are able to move them. When you move them and compromise through strong communication and self assurance, people tend to respect you more, and there's a good chance that even the most stubborn people will meet you halfway. Boundaries exist to protect you, your energy and your happiness, not to isolate you or push people away.

Affirmations

I protect my time and my energy. I have the courage to stand in my power and say 'no' when it suits me.

Action

Identify and write down the people/situations that cause you to feel as though your time and personal space has been invaded. Answer the following questions:

1. How would I like people to treat me?
2. How would I not like people to treat me?
3. I have a right to ask for…
4. To protect my energy, it is perfectly okay for me to…

Limiting Beliefs

You may be feeling a lot of resistance when it comes to dreaming bigger for yourself. From fulfilling, peaceful relationships to nurturing friendships, earning more money and experiencing more joy and fun in life – it's totally natural to feel like it'll never happen for you. When we refer to blocks, what we really mean is that you're probably standing in your own way. I know, it's hard to hear and doesn't make much sense. Why would we ever purposely decide to block ourselves from getting what we want out of life? More often than not, we don't even realise we're doing it. It's our very own subconscious limiting beliefs in action, and the self-fulfilling prophecy that says, 'I'm not going to be/do/have/afford the thing I dream about' because of 'x, y and z'.

To break through your blocks and remove resistance, you need to be fully aware of the reasons and excuses for standing in your own way. We need to make the subconscious, conscious. Once you've done this you can reframe the resistance and find a way to overcome it through empowering affirmations. The aim is to get back in 'flow' and remove the stagnant energy from your heart, mind and body.

Affirmation

I can achieve anything I put my mind to, and I choose to get out of my own way.

Action

Put pen to paper and write absolutely everything you want out of life, without overthinking it. Imagine that anything is possible, and let the words flow from your pen. Take a look at each thing you've written and start to observe your beliefs around it. For example, if you wrote down that you want more money, have a look at your current relationship with your finances. Do you think money is the root of all evil? Do you believe that rich people suck, and there isn't enough money to go around? All of these beliefs are actively blocking money from flowing into your life and therefore we must change your inner world and adapt your beliefs to suit your deepest desires. It's time to start exploring the possibility that money is a good thing, that it can help you with your goals, that having more means you can give more, and then with your new beliefs money will begin to flow into your life. This works with absolutely anything you're wanting to manifest, and overcoming blocks is all about addressing and re-writing your beliefs.

Judgment/Gossip

There's a great quote by author Byron Katie that reads,

"I can find only three kinds of business in the universe: mine, yours, and God's"

Her theory explains that it's both pointless and exhausting to waste your precious energy in God's business, worrying about earthquakes and natural disasters amongst other events that will forever be out of your control. Similarly, if you're constantly talking about other people, concerned with what they're up to, bitching, judging, complaining and 'sticking your nose in', then you are mentally operating in other people's business. And while it might feel satisfying to drag other people down, it really is a sign that you have a lot of work to do on yourself and your own life. This isn't a time to be cruel to yourself and feel guilty – this is a powerful moment of self-awareness where you can make the choice to learn, grow and step into a better version of yourself. When we are aligned with our Inner Queen, our self-esteem and happiness levels are high, and so we are naturally drawn to talking kindly about other people and lifting them up. Moreover, we are far more likely to spend time in our own business; creating magic in our own lives, working on our goals and manifesting our hearts desires.

Affirmation

I stay in my own business and focus on my own goals. I don't need to detract from anyone because I am creating my own magic.

Action

Any time someone near you starts to bitch about someone else, swiftly change the subject and choose not to divulge in the conversation. If you find yourself starting to feel like you want to bitch about someone instead, pause. Wait and see what it is that is coming up in you and why this feeling has come up. Are you trying to fit in? Are you in a circle of people that talk this way regularly? Is the person you are about to talk about doing something that you really want to do? Really try to see why these thoughts have come up and instead of automatically going into bitching mode, instead take a moment to see why you feel the need and what it really is that you need to do instead. Spend less time with bitchy people? Work on your confidence so that you don't feel pressured to join in? Work out why someone makes you feel that way and what you could do for yourself instead?

Completion

The perceived inability to complete on our goals is not an uncommon one. In this day and age of social media and instant gratification, we are hardwired to want immediate results. Our patience wears thin, we refuse to wait around and so we jump from project to project hoping for instantaneous manifestation. So many of us begin a new project with boundless energy, enthusiasm and excitement. In the initial stages we may feel a surge of inspiration, but before long, the self-doubt creeps in. The task ahead seems bigger than we had originally anticipated, there may be obstacles along the way. We begin to question whether it was really a good idea at all. Eventually we procrastinate or give up entirely, it gets buried under a pile of paperwork or filed away for 'another day' and we end up never quite finishing it. We do this time and time again, allowing our lack of patience and relentless self-doubt to sabotage our hopes and dreams, and thus develop a limiting belief that we 'never finish anything!'

The belief that we never finish anything simply isn't true. As humans we tend to cling onto the memories of all the times we never completed a project, and thus develop a self-fulfilling prophecy. You are constantly completing tasks, but never giving yourself credit for them. It's time to realise just how capable you are of finishing the things you started!

Affirmation

I am capable of amazing things and I am choosing to see my projects through to completion.

Action

Grab a pad and write down any tasks or projects you have completed in the last 3 years. This could involve moving to a new house, getting a new job, having a baby, decorating your kitchen or simply reading an entire book. Next, write down all of the projects you'd like to complete, including a list of the tasks you previously abandoned. Put them in order of importance, and then shine a light on what you believe is holding you back from finishing them (be really honest with yourself.) Once you've established the areas in which you're being held back, you can begin to work on problem solving. For example, if one of your reasons is 'I don't have enough time', brainstorm ways in which you can carve out 10 minutes a day to work on your project. Replace your 'all or nothing attitude' with, 'I can get this completed in 6 months if i just do a little bit each day."

Comparison

It was Theodore Roosevelt who said, 'comparison is the thief of joy', and we have to agree with him on this one. Judging ourselves on how well we measure up against other (totally unique) human beings is not only pointless, but results in this painful experience of feeling less than others and has us questioning our own worth. Your Inner Queen never ever questions her own worth. When you're living in alignment with her, you'll stand fully in your power and know that absolutely no other human that has ever or will ever exist can even come close to being as utterly rare as you are. It would be like comparing a sunrise with a blossoming flower, there is absolutely no comparison required. Please take a moment to just appreciate how special you are. Soak it up. Roll around in it. You are the only you that will ever exist. Your talents, gifts, opinions, perceptions, your mind and your body are one of a kind. Nobody else, no matter how hard they try, will ever come close to being you.

Own that.

Affirmation

I am rare, unique and more than enough. I lean into self-acceptance and understand my unbelievable worth.

Action

When you see someone else doing/being/having something great, concentrate on feeling really happy for them. Go out of your way to congratulate them and really focus on how their greatness takes absolutely nothing away from yours. You're untouchable and there's more than enough space for us all in this limitless, never ending Universe.

Control

If you're trying desperately to control every detail of your life, control how others view you and have a tight grip on how you think your life should be unfolding – you're operating in a state of fear. We've got to snap you out of it and bring you back in alignment with your Inner Queen. Remember that she lives in a total state of flow, serenity and trust. The Universe is an incredibly intelligent force of love, do not underestimate the power of letting go, surrendering and allowing life to carry you wherever you need to go. When we lead with our hearts and follow our inner guidance, instead of the incessant, fearful chatter of the mind – we end up aligning with our true path. We allow life to guide us, instead of trying to manipulate and guide life. The unknown can be a daunting concept, we have absolutely no idea what might happen in the next 5 minutes – never mind tomorrow, the day after, or 20 years from now. It's natural to want to keep yourself safe and carefully dictate the outcome of your life, the ego is always trying to find ways to survive no matter what it takes. But your Inner Queen? She just trusts. She's at one with life and chooses to lie back and allow the flow of life to carry her wherever the current takes her.

Affirmation

I surrender to the flow of life, and trust that it will take me wherever I need to go.

Action

Take a moment each morning to close your eyes and visualise yourself lying on your back and floating down a river. Instead of trying to swim upstream against the current of life or cling on to the side of the bank, just allow yourself to let go and enjoy the ride. Look up at the big, blue, beautiful sky above you and feel yourself floating peacefully as the tide carries you along in a state of total trust and surrender.

Confidence

Building confidence in yourself is like training a muscle in the gym. It takes practice, perseverance and the willingness to continuously step out of your comfort zone – over and over again. It takes us to push past our boundaries, break through limiting beliefs and know that we are worthy of speaking our mind and living life on our own terms. Confidence is all about feeling sure of who you are, standing in your power and it really requires the deep understanding that all human beings are equal. It's your birth right to voice your opinion, wear the clothes that make you happy, live in accordance with your own values and stand up for what you believe in. Past experiences such as bullying, rejection, 'embarrassing' experiences and the opinions of others can all cause us to feel self-conscious and insecure. Confident people have a positive mindset, they don't let the opinions of others dictate their choices, and they have a willingness to laugh at themselves when something seemingly 'embarrassing' happens. Confidence is about living with an open heart and comes back again to truly understanding your right to take up valuable space on this earth.

Affirmation

It is safe to step out of my comfort zone and know that I am always enough.
I am brave.
I am strong.
I've got this.

Action

Instead of making decisions from your head where there are fear based thoughts clouding your judgment, close your eyes and focus on your heart. Your Inner Queen is always quietly confident and connecting to your heart space will connect you back to her and help you to make decisions from a place of love.

"What will they think?" "How will that look?" "What do they want me to say?" are all common examples of fear-based thoughts from the mind. When you connect back to your heart, you'll ask questions such as, "What do I really need to say?" "What is the real reason I want to do this?" "How can I be true to myself today?"

Failure

There are two things to focus on when reframing our failures from negative setbacks, into positive opportunities for growth and development.

1. You are human. You were not put on this earth to act out a perfect, immaculate life with impeccable decision-making skills and an existence free from adversity. Your challenges are here to serve you, and we hate to break it to you, but those 'bad' decisions you've made throughout your life have been the very making of you and your character. Each time you take a wrong turn and find yourself questioning your choices, you can sit back and relax, fully aware that you are in a very important period of growth. As the saying goes, "A smooth sea never made a skilled sailor."

So Queen, please trust us when we tell you that those choppy seas are absolutely vital in order for you to master your own life, build your resilience and make better choices in the future. You are learning and you are doing great.

2. You can forgive yourself now. One seemingly 'bad' decision can be left as just that... a bad decision. We can learn from it, move on, and have the self-awareness to never repeat it again. Or, we can beat ourselves up, relive it over and over again in our minds, and then spend the rest of our lives walking around with a heavy and unnecessary cloud of regret hanging over our heads. It's time to forgive yourself, Queen. It's time to accept what happened and really move on, taking the lessons with you and leaving the rest in the past where it belongs.

Affirmation

I am a human being and forgive myself for making mistakes.
There is no such thing as failure if I am constantly learning and upgrading myself.
I am grateful for the challenges.
I am growing.

Action

Take a moment to recall a time where you believe you failed at something. Flip it on it's head, and instead of listing the reasons it didn't work out, try looking for the lessons and growth in it all. What did you learn? How did it shape you as a person? What did it teach you?

Say thank you to the experience, put your hand on your heart and say "I forgive you" to yourself.

Friendships

Friendships play such an important role in our lives. It's important to favour quality over quantity when it comes to our inner circle, so don't worry if you have just one or two people you feel close to. Many of us panic that we're not the popular, social butterflies that society expects us to be, but wouldn't you rather have a deep, meaningful connection with a handful of humans rather than a vague and unpredictable relationship with 30 'mates' that you're unsure if you can fully trust? The people you choose to allow into your space need to be kind, supportive, uplifting and genuine. Make no exceptions. Our friends have the power to impact our life choices, our decision making and our overall happiness, so let's choose wisely. If you are opting to spend time with people who leave you feeling deflated and negative, or people who are constantly gossiping and bringing you down... then it's time to make some serious changes. Your inner Queen is pretty savage about who deserves access to your precious space and time. But she also knows that showing up as your own best friend is absolutely key in order to attract people with similar values to your own. The goal is to create a tribe of likeminded people who are there to hold your hand and help you evolve, just as you do the same for them in return.

But how do we go about making new friends, especially as adults? It can be so daunting to approach another person and ask for their hand in friendship, particularly if they already have a seemingly close-knit circle of mates. The answer really comes down to being genuine, open and confident. Get out of your shell, attend events where you know you'll find people with common interests, talk to those who are on your wavelength and have faith that the right people will find you. Your tribe will come effortlessly when you're being true to yourself.

Affirmations

I surround myself with people who lift me up and inspire me to grow.

I am open to meeting new people and make friends easily.

I cut out toxic people from my life and remove myself from friendships that do not serve my highest good.

Action

In order to assess your current friendships and bring awareness to whether they are serving you, you can rate them on a scale of 0-10. (Zero being friendships that leave you feeling confused, bring drama to your life and have you questioning your worth. Ten being friendships that make you feel completely supported, alive and wholesome.) Any friendships that score below a five, require your strength to address issues head on with them, and the self-assurance to walk away.

Forgiveness

So often people have this tendency to disregard the possibility of forgiveness, because they consider it to be a sign of weakness. They think such an act would mean they're 'giving in', they 'have no backbone' and that by holding a grudge they're punishing the person who wronged them. Far from it. In fact, the polar opposite. Forgiveness is love and every little, wonderful thing in between. It is empathy and compassion, bravery and strength. From forgiveness stems the capacity for rebirth, the opportunity to find freedom and the chance to discover inner peace. (And if you're saying you wouldn't want that then, quite frankly Queen, you're telling porkies.) Without forgiveness there would be nothing but unfinished business, hostility and a never-ending, exhausting cycle of revenge. Don't get me wrong, true forgiveness, the kind that comes from the very bottom of your heart, can take a lot of work. And while it's nowhere near as simple as flicking an on/off switch, it remains a choice. Forgiveness doesn't mean that the person who caused you so much pain is in the right. Nor does it condone what they did. If your best mate slept with your boyfriend, forgiving them doesn't say "It's fine! Let's arrange for the 3 of us to go for dinner next week. And in the meantime, carry on!" Forgiveness simply says, "You hurt me, and I'm not happy about it, but I choose to set myself free of this torment and move on, with no desire to seek revenge as I respect myself far too much to even consider sinking to your level."

Affirmation

I accept the past and choose to let go of anger, resentment and hatred towards myself and others.
I move forward with love in my heart.
Forgiveness is a gift to me.

Action

Make one step towards forgiveness today. Whether it's somebody you haven't spoken to in years, a friend that hurt you yesterday, or even if it's for yourself. Accept the past for what it is, and work towards letting it go. You could send them a text, give them a call or arrange to meet up. If you can't or don't want to interact with them directly, take some time to write a letter to them. Once you have done this you can rip it up or burn it. This is an empowering energetic release.

Fear

Whilst fear is actually a really useful, primitive emotion designed to activate our fight or flight response when faced with a dangerous or life threatening situation, the reality is that we're no longer living as cavemen and we're definitely not exposed to the threat of having our caves raided by hungry boars on a daily basis. Why then, are so many of us choosing to live in a constant state of adrenaline fuelled dread over what happened 6 months ago, or what might happen tomorrow? The answer my Queen, is because of the trusty ol' ego. Whilst the ego exists to keep us safe, using it to guide us through life is going to result in a pretty miserable existence.

The ego always, always wants more. Nothing is ever good enough. The next best car, the next new iPhone, more money, to lose 10lbs, to gain 10lbs, to find the perfect relationship. Only once the ego eventually arrives at any of these goals, it simply isn't satisfied. The ego is never satisfied and will always leave you wanting more. By living a life devoted to achieving what we haven't already, we are living a life based on thoughts of scarcity and lack. Therefore, If our thoughts create our reality, we will continue to exist in the mindset of never truly having enough for the rest of our lives and always live from a place of fear.

Affirmation

When I feel fearful, I recognise that it's just my ego trying to keep me safe.
I stand in my power, know that I am brave and choose to trust the Universe.

Action

Acknowledge your fears. You may have heard this one before. "Fight your fears and you'll be in battle forever; Face your fears and you'll be free forever." Fighting your fears is incredibly counterproductive, as is beating yourself up for having them in the first place. Before we can eliminate them from our lives for good, we must first recall exactly what it is you're afraid of, and make a list of all the things you're afraid of.

Time for a visualisation

Once you're feeling relaxed and comfortable, bring one of the fears you listed to the forefront of your mind. Give the fear a colour and shape. Talk to your fear, out loud or in your head is fine, and thank it for trying to protect you. (This will help you to feel like the fear really is on your side and is only trying to be a friend by protecting you. By being kind to your fears, you are being kind to yourself by removing the resistance associated with them.) Once you have thanked your fear, tell it that you no longer need it, and imagine it floating away. (This is why it's good to give it a colour and shape, because the more vivid the visualisation – the more powerful it will be.)

Heartbreak

The end of a relationship can often feels like you've lost a part of yourself. It's a gruelling process. It hurts. You are growing. But no matter how much your heart aches, you feel like you can't breathe, and you just don't know what to do with yourself – I need you to always remember the most important thing. You are growing. Nothing can take that away from you. It's the most positive thing that you can take from every challenge life throws at you, and trust me – your personal growth is the most important thing in the world. Cherish that. This experience is a vital puzzle piece and a significant part of your beautiful story. Although it feels like it, it really isn't the end of the world. New beginnings are often disguised as painful endings – it's up to you how you choose to look at your situation. As Wayne Dyer famously said, "If you change the way you look at things, the things you look at change." This is a blessing in disguise, we promise.

Understand that you never belonged to each other. It can be really easy to get wrapped up in this idea that when you're in a relationship you 'own' each other and become one. You own nothing in this life, especially not people. You are born into this world empty handed, and you leave empty handed. You don't even get to take your body with you – it returns to Mother Earth where it came from. You just borrow everything for your time here, and you will never, ever own anyone.

The worst thing you can do is try to avoid the pain. You can choose to be reckless. Drink, smoke, stay out all night and pretend you're happy and having fun, but the truth is that this behaviour is a form of escapism. When it comes to dating straight away, sleeping with other people in order to feel close to someone and texting other people for validation or attention, it can feel really relieving to distract yourself, but It means you'd rather avoid your emotions than face them head on. This is time for you. Time to focus your energy on loving yourself and putting yourself first. If you feel rejected, it's because you need more self-acceptance. You need YOU right now above all other people, a cuddle from your friends and going home to see your family will work wonders. But until you give yourself the love you're craving in order to feel whole again, you'll continue to feel sort of empty and lost. Please don't neglect yourself.

Affirmation
I am whole on my own.
I am strong enough to overcome anything.
This is a blessing in disguise.

Action

Mirror work – look deep into your own eyes and say 'I love you' every day. After saying it smile. Even though this practice can feel uncomfortable to begin with, please stick with it. It will start to become easier and over time it will have a profound effect on your sense of self-love by deepening your connection with your Inner Queen and nurturing the most important relationship in your life.

Jealousy

In a world where everybody wants to follow the crowd by looking, dressing and acting in a way that society deems as 'acceptable'- please choose to go against the grain and see the beauty in your individuality. When you experience feelings of jealousy, it means that you're longing for something that somebody else has, and this takes you away from acceptance of all that you are. If acceptance is the answer to inner peace, then jealousy can be found at the root of deep inner turmoil. It's an incredibly uncomfortable emotion, and one that can have quite a toxic impact on your relationship with yourself and with others. Looking to other people for inspiration is healthy and completely normal, but to look at someone else's life and feel envious isn't, and it's something that requires a whole load of self-awareness so we can address this fear-based emotion head on. The most important thing to remember is that no matter how successful, fabulous, beautiful or inspiring you consider another human to be – not even a fraction of their greatness can take away your own. You're untouchable, because you are completely and utterly unique. Pitching yourself against another person is an act of the ego and requires us to judge ourselves and others as either 'better' or 'worse' than one another. But your Inner Queen knows that there is no comparison needed. One of the most beautiful things you could ever do is choose to stand in your own power, know your own unique and incredible worth, and relax – safe in the knowledge that you are enough. Exactly as you are.

The energy that this level of self-assurance gives off has its own extremely alluring power. A Queen that knows who she is and is able to empower other women without feeling as though it takes anything away from her sense of worthiness, is a powerful force of love. Jealousy is an ugly trait derived from the ego's constant need to have, be and do more in order to feel superior to others.

Affirmations

I am enough, exactly as I am.

I connect to my Inner Queen and know that nobody else's greatness can ever take away my own.

I understand my worth and empower other women because we are all unique.

Action

When a feeling of envy or jealousy arises within you, take a moment to sit with the emotion. Welcome it in. What is trying to teach you? Which parts of you are you failing to accept whilst longing for what somebody else has? Think about can you take inspiration from this experience and relax into a feeling of deep love and acceptance for yourself.

Loneliness

"Connection is the energy that exists between people when they feel seen, heard and valued; when they can give and receive without judgement; and when they derive sustenance and strength from the relationship." —Brené Brown,

We require social connection to survive, it's a core human need and meaningful friendships help us to feel loved, valued and cared for. There are so many reasons that we might find ourselves isolated and alone, from moving to a new house, starting a new job, lacking the money to join in with social events, to going through a breakup or bereavement. In these instances, feeling human connection is about getting out into the world and making new friendships, having the confidence to approach people and joining in more social events. You may want to try volunteering, being of service to others, reconnecting with old friends or trying a new creative class where you can meet some friendly and likeminded people.

But the feeling of loneliness can also be present when we are surrounded by others. It's entirely possible to be living in a city with millions of people or in a room filled with acquaintances, in a relationship or surrounded by friends – and still somehow feel a deep sense of loneliness. When this happens, it really means that we are disconnected from ourselves and is a sign of misalignment with our inner world. So how do we reconnect with ourselves, and begin to feel less detached?

Your Inner Queen knows that she is never alone, for she is always connected to the Universe, or Source Energy where she understands that we are all one. Everything in this entire Cosmos is connected, including you and I. You are not separate or some kind of exception to the rule, you do not stand alone on this planet. You are part of Mother Nature, and so you will always belong here. Loneliness is an emotion, and it's definitely not who you are. It doesn't define you, and while it may feel all-consuming – it can never ever become you. Loneliness is separate from you, and when you make friends with yourself and connect back to your Inner Queen you will feel a deep sense of inner peace and contentment. It was Dr. Wayne Dyer who said, "You'll never be alone if you like the person you're alone with."

Sitting in your own company with no distractions and really, truly making friends with the person looking back at you in the mirror is the ultimate way to cure loneliness. The voice in your head needs to be warm and kind, and you must be willing to become your own best friend first. This takes time, commitment and nurturing.

Affirmation

I am open to receiving more connection in my life and I make a conscious effort to connect with others.

I am becoming my own best friend.

I value my time alone.

I enjoy my own company and feel safe in my own presence.

Action

Connect back to your mind and body through movement or meditation. Become your own best friend, and work on creating positive, gentle and uplifting self-talk. Taking yourself to a new dance class or volunteering somewhere may just be the answer you're looking for. Other creative outlets such as painting, singing and writing might also help. Choose something that lights you up and connects you back to yourself.

Loss

Losing something we once had, whether it be a person, an animal, a relationship, our home, belongings or job can be incredibly difficult to process. As humans it's very natural that we become attached to people, things, situations and circumstances – but it's important to recognise that attachment actually leads to suffering. Why? Because ultimately, change is the only constant in this Universe. Nothing lasts forever, but the world around us is constantly transforming. Just as the seasons change, the tides move, the planets spin, the sun rises and falls – life too has an extremely beautiful way of being in a constant state of renewal. The thing is, since we come into this world with no belongings, and we can't take anything with us when we die, all of the stuff we accumulate during our time here is merely borrowed. Nothing is ever really ours to own. This perspective alone can remove a lot of suffering, and we can relax knowing that people, things and circumstances will flow in and out of our lives as and when they please. The key is to loosen our grip on life. If somebody wants to leave, let them. If you are fired from your job, walk away and trust that it was meant to happen. As the saying goes, when one door closes, another one really does open. And when that door opens it will reveal our next chapter, maybe it's a new period of growth, a new person, a new career or opportunity. Accept the past for what it was, thank the Universe for the experience and move forward in a state of surrender. What's meant for you will not pass you by.

Affirmation

Nothing in this world is mine to own, I loosen my grip on life and live in a state of flow.

I am grateful for my past and accept that change is the only constant.

Action

Hold space for yourself to grieve the loss you've experienced and give yourself time to process the emotion. List all of the good things that came from the experience you once had and fill yourself with gratitude for it all. Repeat your affirmations and lean into acceptance.

Feeling Overwhelmed

If you're feeling overwhelmed it's a sure sign that you need to slow down and take a moment for stillness and silence. When we take on too much at once, when we're trying to balance our work life, social life, nurture our relationships, drink enough water, socialise, read, work on ourselves (the list goes on and on), it's only natural to feel like life is trying to swallow you whole. Please give yourself a break, Queen. Please take the pressure off and stop trying to do it all. It has been said that we are human beings, not human doings. It's perfectly fine for you to cut down your commitments, start saying 'no' more often and spend more time relaxing and taking care of yourself. It's time to set some boundaries, slow down and commit to daily meditation in place of some of the less important tasks you feel obliged to complete.

Affirmations

I am doing my best and my best is always enough.
I deserve time out to relax and reconnect with myself.
I have got this.

Action

Take 3 deep breaths, come back to the present moment and remember how capable you are. You've totally got this. Before you start your day, take 10 minutes to sit in silence or do a guided meditation. Get yourself in a positive and calm mindset before you take on any of your tasks. Make a list of what needs to be done. Put your to do list in order of priority, and then handle one thing at a time.

Say 'no' the people, things and situations that you cannot handle right now.

Overthinking

There is no such thing as a present moment thought, so if you're lost in the world of overthinking, you can be sure that you're either mentally living in the past or daydreaming about the future. Either way, getting tangled up in this thinking trap is the ultimate route to feeling anxious, worried and stressed out. Many of our uncomfortable thoughts about the past or future come as a result of trying to manipulate, control or resist our own lives. When we resist, we argue with reality, and the never-ending cycle of discontentment ensues. The ultimate cure for overthinking is practising meditation, and repeatedly coming back to the present moment where there is nothing but peace, tranquillity, acceptance and love. The goal is to co-exist peacefully with your thoughts, and make sure that your inner dialogue is reassuring, supportive and kind.

Affirmations

Any time I feel myself slip into overthinking; I choose to come back to the present moment.

I understand that neither the past nor future exist, and this present moment is all I need to focus on.

I am not my thoughts.

Action

Author, Sandy Newbigging, talks about some methods for meditation practice and has a very useful and easy exercise you can do in order to come back into the present moment. Let's take the room or place you're in right now an example. There might be a sofa you're sitting on, furniture, a lamp. Maybe you're outside surrounded by trees. For all of these things to exist and have a place in the world, they need the space around them to hold them there. And although the physical things will come and go over time; the trees will change with the seasons, your furniture will change as people move in and out of your home over the years – one thing always remains constant. The space between everything.

It's ever present, it never changes, never leaves, never makes a sound. In order to come back into the present moment, take a few minutes to focus on the space around you, filling the gaps between the physical items. Hold your attention gently on the space around you and feel yourself filling up with a deep sense of inner peace.

Practice this every time you feel yourself slip into overthinking.

Purpose

The Universe has an extraordinarily generous and fascinating way of planting seeds of unlimited creativity within us all; then it cheers us on as we try (or don't try) to uncover them. And what you need to recognise is that the journey to finding those tiny little nuggets of potential is exactly why we are here. Exploring, questioning, playing, listening, and experimenting, all in the hope of unearthing these God-given gifts. And the courage needed to travel the road of self-discovery and find your purpose, is the very thing that will determine just how mundane or awesome your time here on this earth will be. It's in your hands. Make the decision today to live the inspired life that is absolutely, indisputably your birth right. Do the things that fill you up, the things that take you to that headspace where nothing else matters, where hours can pass and yet feel like only minutes... That's where it's at. Which gifts are you ignoring for fear of not being good enough? One single little act of creativity will help to bring forward the real, authentic you and help you to unleash your Inner Queen. Discover what's in there! You never know what you might find.

Affirmations

I find my sense of purpose in doing the things that truly fill me with joy.
I trust my path and know I am always being guided by the Universe.

Action

Write down the answers to the following questions. What did you want to be when you were younger? Why was this? If money wasn't an issue, what would your dream job be? How can you be of service to others?

Self-worth

Queen, it's time to realise your worth. My Goodness, you are incredible! It's so important to remember that there is only one of you, in all of time! How long is time? It's never-ending. It's infinite. And there is ONE OF YOU. And there has never and will never live another like you. Each of us has a multitude of gifts so ridiculously unique, it would be impossible for them to be replicated by someone else. You do not have to be the greatest singer, or poet, or chef, or actor, in the entire world in order to make your mark here on earth. You are just as important as Beyoncé, or Walt Whitman, Heston Blumenthal or Al Pacino.

Your worth is not defined by fame, beauty, money, awards or popularity. The homeless guy sitting on the corner of your street has exactly the same worth as the Queen of England. He is a human being, as is she. And at the end of the day, that is all that matters. Knowing your worth and loving yourself is the most important thing in the world. From here stems nothing but opportunity for peace, love, joy and inspiration, and that's why it's my first step. Recognise that you deserve more. Recognise that you are worthy of unlimited abundance and happiness, every single day…and recognise that the only thing holding you back from it – is yourself.

Affirmation
I deserve to live a magical life filled with adventure and excitement.
I am infinitely worthy of my own love. I am one of a kind.

Action
Make a point of saying 'I love myself' whilst looking in the mirror and then smile. It can feel totally alien saying this at first and can make a lot of people feel really uncomfortable even keeping eye contact with themselves. Please stick with it. There comes a point when this starts to feel easier and then a time will come when you see your own reflection and your natural response will be to smile and feel love. This may seem like a really small action but we promise it will make a huge change to your life over time.

Self-Talk

The way we talk to ourselves is so unbelievably important. It's the very foundation on which we build a beautiful, joyful and fulfilling life. This entire journal has been designed to help you cultivate a kind, gentle and confident inner voice that empowers you to believe in yourself and your ability to create a life you love. If the voice in your head is constantly bullying you, putting you down and telling you how worthless you are – you will continue to live at war with yourself until you decide to change your inner dialogue. How are you ever going to create a life that feels good if the world's worst flatmate is renting space in your head? Your mind needs to be on your side. You need to become your own best friend, you need to champion your Inner Queen and this isn't up for debate. If you only take one thing from this entire journal, let this be it.

Affirmation

I am committed to becoming my own best friend.
I practice kind, loving thoughts every single day.
I am my own biggest cheerleader.

Action

Complete this journal daily and honour your Inner Queen. Say your affirmations every time you look in the mirror when going to the bathroom. Repeat them silently if you are in public but do make sure to do them consistently. This is training your brain to automatically think uplifting thoughts, and new habits take time to build. Show up for yourself, you really do deserve it.

IF YOU MAKE FRIENDS WITH YOURSELF, YOU WILL NEVER BE ALONE.

Dear Jodi,

What a year it's been!! 2020 has thrown some hurdles, yet here you are, surviving (just) and ready to embark on a journey of growth + self development. Before we do that, we need to address the last 12 months truthfully + honestly.

In Sept '19, you gave birth to a beautiful baby girl. She was healthy + thrived, yet you missed your old life + quickly lost your identity. I'm here to tell you that this is <u>normal</u>!!! She cried ALOT, you felt isolated, alone, guilty + exhausted. You felt bored, which made you feel more guilty + you cried, equally as much. You battled through + gave 100% of yourself to Ida, every, single, day. This made you more tired + drained your spark. Please do not feel hard on yourself. Your love for her, made you forget to love yourself. Now we can change that.

You became anxious + nervous to be too far of home for an irrational fear that something could happen to her. You began cancelling plans on the day to cope w/ the enormity of the event. This was a coping mechanism, which you adopted to keep Isla + you safe. Please don't feel defeated or guilty about this. You did not know a global pandemic + total lockdown was just around the corner!

It is generally agreed you have a level of PTSD from those early weeks, unsurprising as you battled early motherhood relatively single-handedly, w/ Rich working long hours + the flat, a cause for isolation. You did your absolute best everyday, pushing yourself to go to baby groups + socialise w/other new mums, who all seemed to have their shit together! You were a good friend throughout, offering support to other mums, a confidant to old friends + sounding board to work colleagues. You found it hard to return texts, but even when if it took a few days, you always did eventually.

You fled family from afar + felt heartbroken that your Dad was fairly absent. You felt resentful of Rich. How does is it fair that his life wouldn't change but I'd lose who I was completely?! He did everything for both of you but you still intrinsically felt it was never enough. By Christmas, people were telling you it all gets much easier @ this age + you smiled as you chugged that extra glass of wine to cope w/the thoughts that everyday was becoming increasingly more difficult. The sleep deprivation eating away @ your sparkle. But your total, all-consuming, unconditional love kept you showing up for her as each dawn broke. You hired a sleep consultant, resulting in worse sleep because you never gave up. The nap battles, the rocking, the endless squatting was were behind you, because you kept going. In March

Printed in Great Britain
by Amazon

45312126R00140